Take Silk

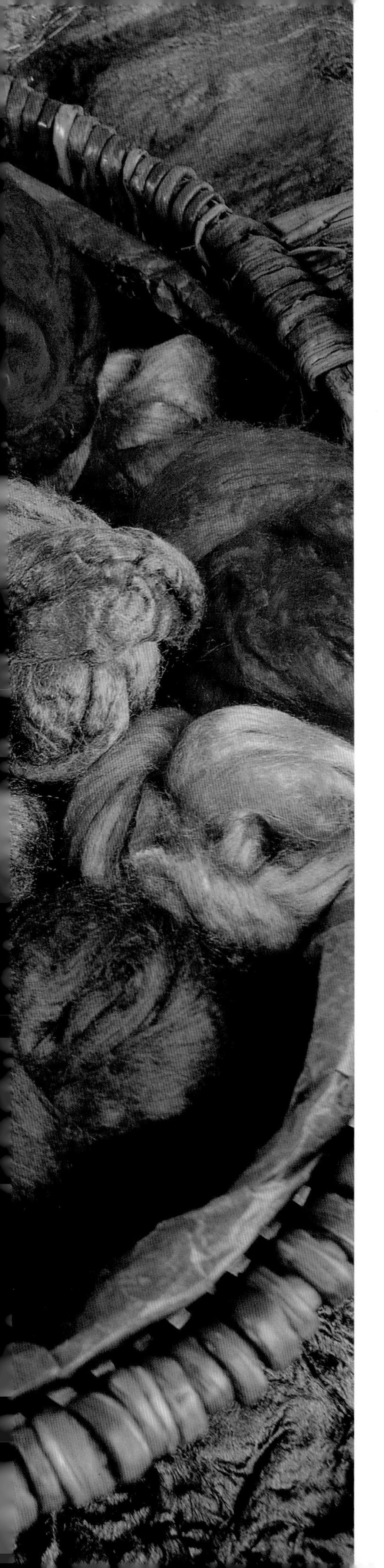

Take Silk

A Guide to Silk 'Paper' for the Creative Fibre Artist

Judith Pinnell

SEARCH PRESS

First published in Great Britain in 2002
by Search Press Ltd
Wellwood
North Farm Road
Tunbridge Wells
Kent TN2 3DR

First published in Australia 2001
by Sally Milner Publishing Pty Ltd
PO Box 2104
Bowral NSW 2576

ISBN 1 903975 24 7

Design by Vivien Valk
Editing by Lyneve Rappell
Illustrations and diagrams by Judith Pinnell
Photography by Bewley Shaylor
Styling by Judith Pinnell and Bewley Shaylor

Disclaimer

Printed in Hong Kong

A practical craft book from Search Press

To Martin

Acknowledgments

I would like to acknowledge the following people who have helped me make this book happen. Nancy Ballesteros, for introducing me to silk 'paper' and who dyes the beautiful silk tops that I use in my work; Bewley Shaylor, for his excellent photography; Caroline and Lucy for so graciously modelling the garments; Peggy Buckingham, Valerie Campbell-Harding and Kristen Dibbs for their generous help and encouragement; Karen Selk for allowing me to reproduce her information of the beginnings of silk; and the contributing artists Kristen Dibbs, Lois Ives, Celia Player, Thyra Roberston, Dale Rollerson and Karen Selk for adding an extra dimension to the work presented.

Contents

Judith Pinnell

Judith Pinnell was born and educated in Australia. She lived in the UK for 29 years where she obtained the City and Guilds Diploma in Design and Embroidery and attended various courses in textile dyeing.

Returning to Perth in 1983 she embarked on 'a journey of discovery' by becoming involved in machine embroidery. She began teaching in Perth, rural Western Australia and interstate, concentrating mainly on machine embroidery, and developing an all-consuming love for colour and texture. Seven years ago she 'discovered' silk 'paper' and the rest, as they say, is history.

She has work in private collections and has exhibited within Australia (National Craft Award Darwin), the USA, New Zealand and the UK. She has had work published in The Bernina International Calendar (Switzerland) 1995, and in Fiberarts Book Five (USA). The most recent publication has been in Machine Embroidery: Inspiration from Australian Artists by Kristen Dibbs.

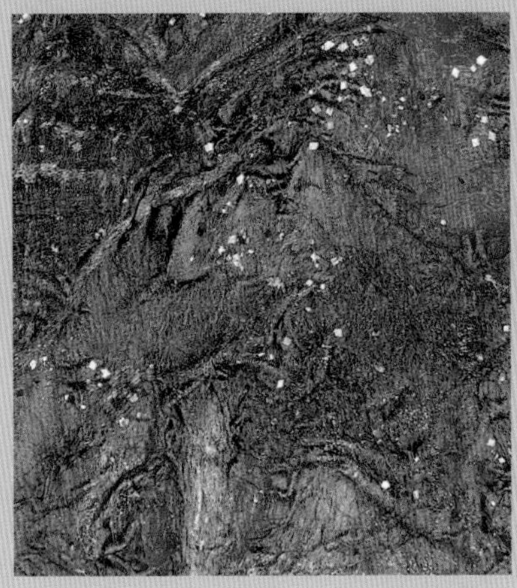

ABOVE: Container, with a curved lid. Free machine embroidery, machined mirror work, beaded tassel

FAR LEFT: Detail – 'Bhuj Remembered' Appliqué with metallic threads and fabrics

LEFT: Open work—lace and inlaying of glitter on the surface

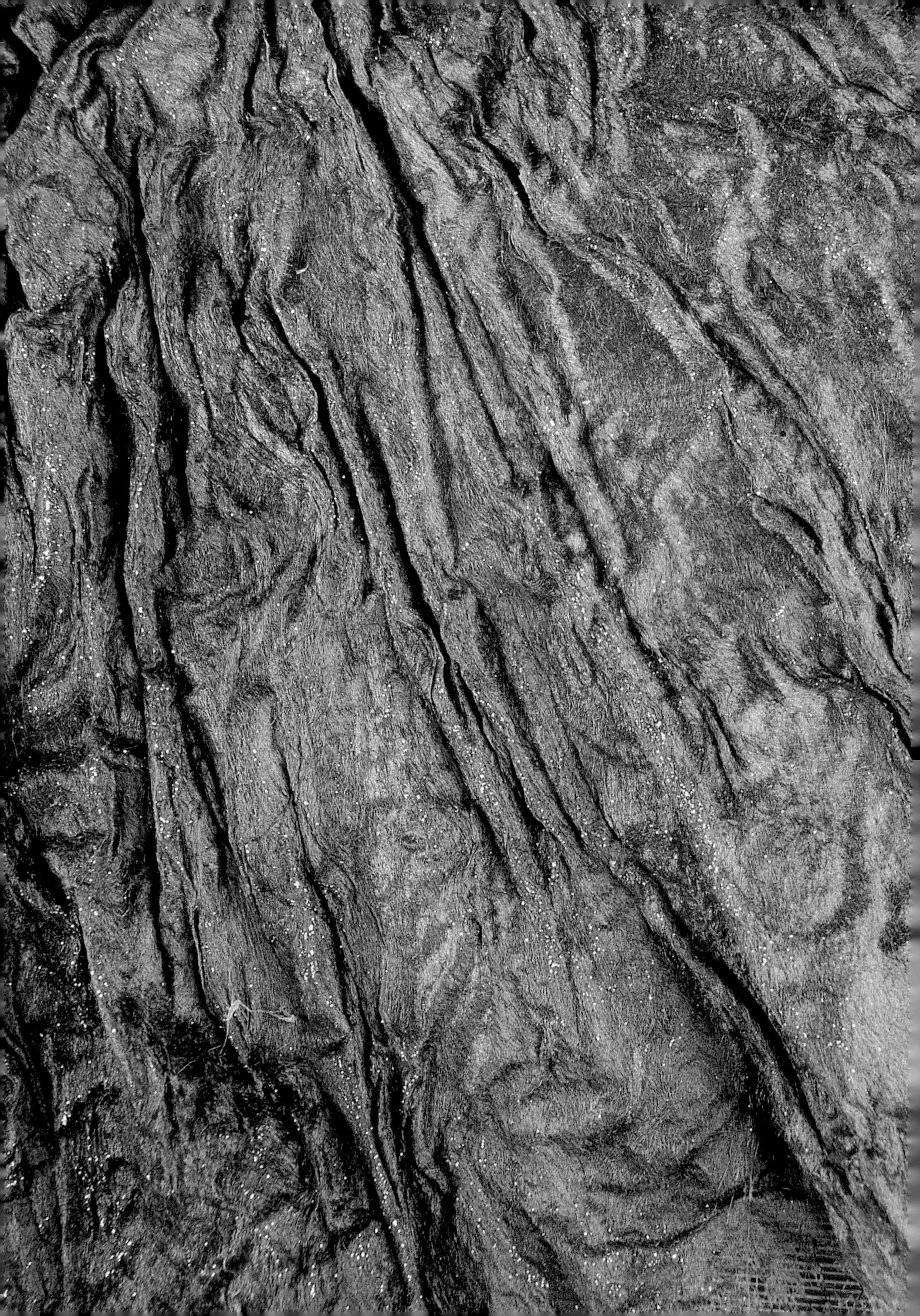

Introduction

Silk 'Paper'

The process of making the silk 'paper' is simple and results in a colourful and lustrous substrate from which you can create a myriad of exciting projects.

As I work predominantly with a sewing machine, I have aimed to interest and excite machine embroiderers. However, if you love rich colours, the feel of silk and have a desire to create, then silk 'paper' is for you. Both traditional and hand embroiderers will find plenty to interest them; to experiment on, using rich threads and other accessories; with which to create two- and three-dimensional pieces that are completely original.

Raw silk is processed and sold in many forms. Unspun dyed silk or silk 'tops' are strong and yield the best results for making silk 'paper'. Using these and a simple forming process, you can create a substrate (base material) with many of the characteristics of both paper and felt, and with the rich lustre that only silk can produce.

TOP: Some of the beautifully coloured silk tops available

ABOVE: Samples of dyed silk

OPPOSITE: Covered notebooks, neck-piece, elephant brooches embellished with beads and rich fabrics

The texture of silk 'paper' is similar to both paper and felt, but as silk is non-porous and does not felt, it cannot be called felted silk. The name silk 'paper' seems the most accurate description for the finished substrate. Instead of using the traditional papermaking equipment of a mould and deckle, a simple process similar to felt making is used. One, two or three layers of silk fibres are laid down and wetted. Adhesive is applied to bind the fibres together. When completely dry, the sheet of silk 'paper' is ready to work on.

Silk 'paper' offers great scope for creativity as a base for machine and hand embroidery. Working in two or three dimensions, limited only by imagination and inspiration, any of the following can be made: bags, jewellery, hats, garments, theatrical masks, brooches, book covers (loose and fitted), bowls, containers and wall hangings. Many areas are yet to be explored.

Experience the satisfaction of making not only your own substrate, but with embellishment and imagination, producing a totally original and individual creation.

How I Began

I was introduced to silk 'paper' in 1992. Nancy Ballesteros, of 'Treetops' Colour Harmonies, returned from a visit to the USA where she had seen the technique in its experimental stage. Her demonstration convinced me that here was an exciting new textile medium worth pursuing in my line of contemporary machine embroidery.

For nearly two years, Nancy experimented with various bonding mediums to find just the right one for the silk fibres, while I worked on the 'paper', testing its durability as a substrate for embroidery. At this time, the adhesives were still in the experimental stage, so anything we made was kept for our own records.

As a contemporary embroiderer, I was keen to try the various techniques that I had been using on conventional fabrics with my machine. I found that if I had a two-layer sheet of 'paper' it was heavy enough not to require the use of a frame, so free machining—with the feed teeth down and using the darning foot—was easy.

I found it was important to use a thin needle, a 10 or 12 (70-80), certainly no thicker, as a larger needle made hole marks on the 'paper'.

I experimented with quilting, open work and applique. By adding a lightweight batting at the back of the work, quilting was most effective. It was possible to criss-cross and create a spider's web by cutting holes no bigger than 1" (2.5 cm) in diameter without using a frame. It had always been necessary to use a frame when working on conventional fabrics using this technique.

I worked with applique and used machine threads layered on the surface. Using my 'cut off' threads, I stitched them down on to the dried 'paper'. I also laid threads on the surface with a gossamer layer of silk tops prior to the batt being wet down. Once the 'paper' had been wet then dried, the threads had securely adhered to the surface.

My next experiments were with paint and print. The 'paper' accepted paints as easily as conventional paper. I was able to stencil, brush, roll and sponge thick paints onto the 'paper' with satisfying results. Especially interesting finishes were achieved by sponging thick fabric paints lightly onto dry 'paper' that had been textured during its construction. This gave a mottled effect that was great for embellishing with threads and beads.

When constructing collars, I drew up the outline of the collar, laid down a batt to fit the shape and created the 'paper' to the shape of the collar. This gave the outer edge a misty effect, which was much softer than an edge that had been cut with scissors.

I made several three-dimensional articles by making a square of silk 'paper', allowing it to dry, then stencilling with gold paint and machining open work on the sides. I wet the 'paper' again and applied more adhesive. The wet 'paper' was moulded on to an acrylic bowl and pleated to fit. This was a successful exercise, and maybe one day I shall find the time to make a complete set of bowls. I also made a pair of triangular shaped boxes to fit inside each other. These were richly embellished with free machine,

Detail – 'Bhuj Remembered' Appliqué with metallic threads and fabrics

beading, tiny shisha mirrors and silk tassels. It was easy to stitch ribbons, lace, cords, couch wools and thick metallic braids to decorate the surface. Edges could be cut or left with a soft misty look.

After two years of experimenting, I knew that here was a wonderful new substrate, and that there would be no bounds to its creative use.

Silk

The history of silk begins in China. In 2640BC, Se-Ling-She, wife of the fabled 'Yellow Emperor', dropped a cocoon into her tea. It began to unravel. This gave her the idea of unreeling the cocoons into long floating threads of silk. This was, so the story goes, the beginning of silk. Silk production became such an important part of Chinese life that the Empress was later defined as the 'Goddess of Silkworms'.

The symbol of silk was already part of the written language in 2600BC. Fragments of Chinese silk from as early as 1500BC have been found. The oldest written record of the use of the fibres comes from India. The Greeks knew silk fabric as 'woven wind'. The establishment of the Silk Road marked the beginning of an abundance of silk in the West. Today, there are a variety of silk fabrics: damask, chiffon, organza, crepe de chine, tussah, shantung and satin, to name but a few.

The once wild silk moth has been domesticated for nearly 5000 years and has gone through many changes. Through domestication, its body structure has been greatly modified, so it has lost its power of flight and become completely dependent on man for survival.

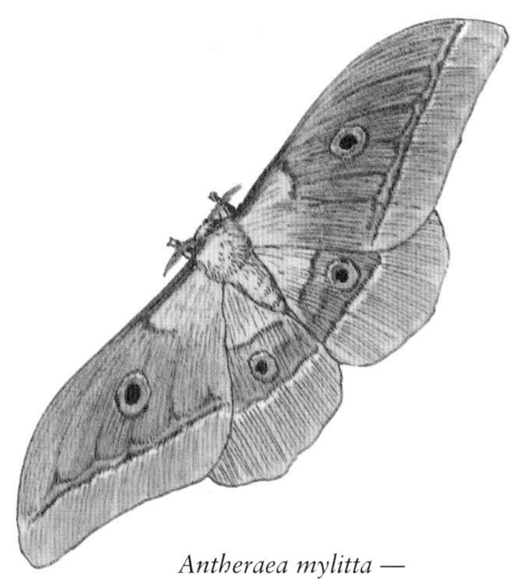

Antheraea mylitta —
Tussah moth

Hyalophora cecropia —
Cecropia moth

Silk moths belong to two families. *Bombycidae*—the commercial silkworm, and *Saturniidae*—the wild silkworm. *Bombyx mori* is the most important variety of the commercial silkworm. It is named *Bombyx* because it belongs to the spinner family of insects, and mori because it normally feeds on the leaves of *Morus alba*—the Chinese white mulberry tree.

The life cycle of the *Bombyx mori* has four stages:

1. Egg
2. Larva (silkworm)
3. Chrysalis or capsule-enclosed pupa (cocoon)
4. Moth, which will lay eggs and begin the cycle again.

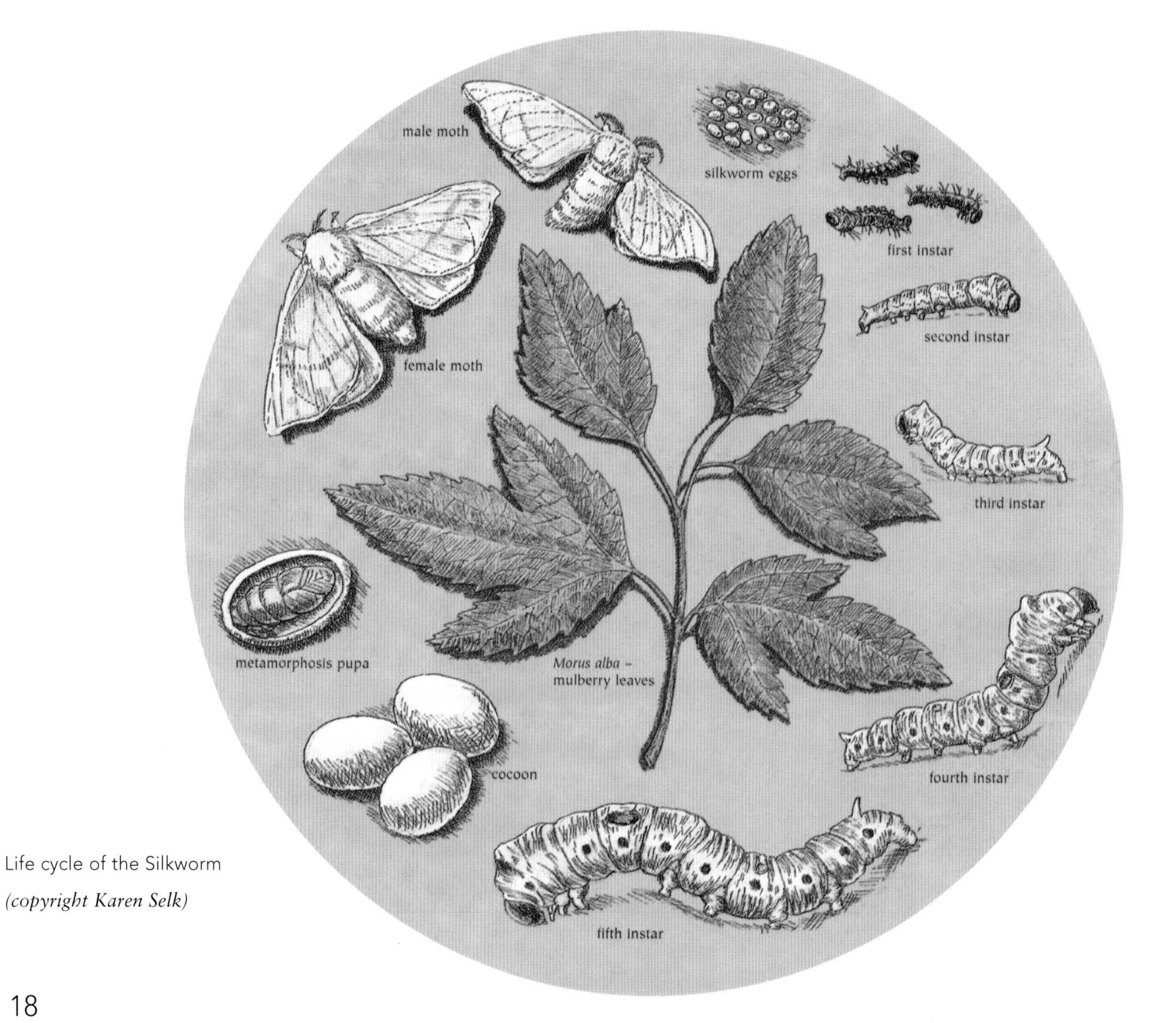

Life cycle of the Silkworm
(copyright Karen Selk)

The best larvae, or silkworms, are selected to produce silk. Rejected larvae are buried where domestic animals cannot eat them, as they cause harmful effects. Alternatively, they are thrown to fish, which thrive on them. Selected larvae are weighed then laid uniformly on specially prepared mats.

Mulberry leaves are the silkworm's sole diet. These are selected at the silk farm, where they are shredded into small pieces and spread on mats of meshed rushes for the insects to feed on. They like a healthy environment, so it is necessary to clean the rushes regularly.

As silkworms sicken easily they require careful, frequent attention and resent being disturbed. Their living quarters need to be kept at an even temperature, as they are sensitive to atmospheric changes. On cold days, fires are lit to warm the air.

When the silkworms reach maturity they are given more space to develop their cocoons. Special care must be taken at this stage to see that nothing goes wrong. Silkworms eat and work as a harmonious body and must not be disturbed while spinning.

When the cocoons are sorted, those selected for further breeding are stored in a cool and well-aired room. The cocoons that will produce the silk are put into earthen jars and covered with layers of leaves and salt to kill the insects without damaging the silk fibres. They are then soaked in copper pots filled with hot water and the cocoons are unwound by reeling the filaments into skeins usually 8 to 10 together. The skeins of silk are dried, wound, and made into reels.

(Based on 'The Silk Saga' by Karen Selk, with her kind permission).

Materials & Equipment

General

- A working space larger than the plastic sheeting being used
- Access to a sink and water
- A selection of silk 'tops' (see 'Suppliers')
- A strong plastic sheet at least 1 yd (1 m) square for preparing the batt and wetting down the silk
- Nylon net, at least 2 yd (2 m), any colour (I prefer black)—avoid using tulle as it tears when being removed from the dry silk 'paper'
- Adhesive solution (see page 22)
- Apron and rubber gloves (optional)
- Sponges or old towelling or flannels to soak up excess water and suds
- Strong washing up liquid
- Two 2–3″ (5–8 cm) wide, cheap household paint brushes for applying medium and water
- An iron
- Two or three small glass or plastic bowls or interesting shaped containers suitable for moulding silk (not your best acrylics as they can be damaged by the medium)
- A hairdryer for use when moulding bowls and three dimensional pieces
- Two or three large yoghurt pots or take-away containers to hold soapy solution and adhesive—these can be throwaways
- A drying frame (see page 25)
- A bucket or similar container for washing out the net after use

JO SONJA'S
TEXTILE MEDIUM
FOR FABRIC PAINTING
250mL
Atelier
ACRYLIC GLOSS
MEDIUM & VARNISH
250 ML

Adhesives

There are many art supply companies that produce various types of adhesive medium. It is important to understand that each company has its own formula that may or may not work well with the silk.

Atelier's Acrylic Gloss Medium/Varnish by Chroma Acrylics is an adhesive which stiffens the silk enough for sculpting, but still leaves it easy to stitch by hand or machine. Follow the manufacturers instructions, but it is usual to mix the solution with equal amounts of water—a 50/50 mix.

If the dry 'paper' appears to require more body for the project in hand, it is possible to paint on more solution after the paper has dried. If too little adhesive has been used the surface of the 'paper' will be fuzzy, with loose silk on the surface. Simply brush on more adhesive, let it dry and proceed to embellish the 'paper'. It is, however, very difficult to machine or stitch on a stiff surface so do the stitching on the dried silk before adding more Acrylic Gloss Medium to save many broken needles. If you would like a very stiff surface, dry the paper with a hairdryer.

The adhesive cannot be removed once it has dried. Iron out any wrinkles once the silk 'paper' is dry using a medium-to-hot iron and a presser cloth or brown paper.

Brushing on more adhesive when the 'paper' is dry does not leave a watermark when using this medium.

To add a new layer of silk 'paper' to an existing piece, brush a small quantity of washing up liquid and water, then some more adhesive to the dry 'paper' to soften the surface. Then lay more silk tops on to the first sheet. Continue laying down the silk tops until you have the desired result. Be sure to use the same adhesive, as only this medium will adhere to itself.

A sheet of 'paper' made with *Jo Sonja's Textile Medium* by Chroma Acrylics is water repellent within limits (experiment) and is excellent for wearable art. The paper is quite flexible and lustrous but has a slightly coated feel and does not 'rub' up as easily as 'paper' made with the Acrylic Gloss Medium.

This solution is used undiluted. You can experiment with diluting it, but the 'paper' will be very soft and have less strength. To ensure proper bonding, follow the manufacturer's instructions. Press the dry 'paper' using a medium-to-hot iron under a press cloth or brown paper, before using. If I have a large sheet to be pressed I take it to the dry cleaners, who kindly press it for me. Too little adhesive will allow the layers to bubble and possibly separate. This may or may not be a problem depending on your use of the 'paper'. By machining or hand stitching into your 'paper' you can reinforce the surface and turn a possible useless piece of 'paper' into a challenge for stitching.

If you add more Textile Medium to 'paper' that has been made with Textile Medium, you will be left with a watermark.

Some uses for paper made with this adhesive include: applique, bags (very suitable), purses, wearable art, hats, belts, books, notepad covers and anything that is handled a lot. When an article is in use, any stains can be removed by gently sponging the 'paper' with a dampened cloth.

Remember, the two adhesives are not compatible with one another and should not be mixed, either wet or dry.

Methylcellulose is a temporary adhesive, sizing and internal stiffener, which is used by papermakers. Use Dow Methocel A4C (approximately 5 tspn per 4 cups water) or CMC Methylcellulose (approximately 5 tblspns per 4 cups of water), and always follow the manufacturers instructions (1 cup=250 ml). You can purchase these powders from most handmade paper suppliers. It is very important to use the pure archival quality brands for longevity of your piece. The paste can be thinned or thickened according to the stiffness you desire in the paper. However, too much paste can cause an undesirable glossing effect, so experiment.

Chemically, methylcellulose is constantly absorbing atmospheric moisture and expanding microscopically. It is, therefore, not stable. A piece made with this medium will begin quite stiff then soften up over time. Eventually the adhesive will almost disappear. It is recommended only for use when the piece will be contained under glass, or heavily reinforced with stitching. When used with felting the methylcellulose washes out.

PVA Glue can be used, but I do not like the glossy surface that results.

Ormaline Fabric Medium may also be used. Once again the finished results are not as pleasing as when using the Textile Medium or Acrylic Gloss.

The choice of adhesive is very personal and you may find, on experimentation, that one of the above may work well for you and your projects. So, experiment and look for new adhesives that might serve your purpose just as well as the ones I use.

Drying Frames

Do not leave your silk 'paper' to dry on the plastic. It will accumulate excess solution and dry with a shiny surface. Dry your silk 'paper' on one of the following frames:

- drip-drying tray (see page 26) when making small pieces
- an old screen-printing frame (not your best one—it will never be the same again)
- an old wire door or window screen (if you have space for it!)
- two or three fine mesh cake cooling racks will do when you first start or for making small pieces.

If you are unable to dry your silk 'paper' outside, try one of the following indoor methods:

- a drip-drying tray
- suspend your drying frame over a sink or basin
- using cake cooling racks or a frame, spread a plastic sheet and plenty of newspapers on the floor and allow the excess medium to drain away.

My homemade frames are very simple: a pine frame stapled together with fine nylon netting stretched over the frame, similar to a silkscreen frame. A useful size is 20½ in x 28½ in (52 cm x 72 cm).

To make a Drip-Drying Frame

Materials

- A large shallow tray 2″ (5 cm) deep, e.g. a cake tin, shallow baking dish or a strong shallow cardboard box from a supermarket
- Plastic sheet, strong cling film or wide aluminium foil—enough to line the dish or box on the sides and bottom
- Flywire, fibreglass net or nylon netting
- Clips to hold the lining in, e.g. bulldog clips, clothes pegs or strong, wide, sticky tape

Method

1. Completely line the tray or dish with plastic, cling film or foil.
2. Secure around the edges with clips, pegs or tape.
3. Stretch wire or netting to cover over the top of the tray or dish.
4. Secure the lining with clips or tape.

The drip-drying Frame is now ready to take your wet silk ‘paper’. It is suitable for small pieces.

How to Make Silk 'Paper'

It is a simple process to make silk 'paper'. Please enjoy working with these rich fibres and beautiful colours. The rules are few and once you have mastered the technique you will be able to experiment and put your individual stamp on the silk 'paper'.

Materials

Silk tops (a top that has been carded and combed to align fibres of specified length)—to make two medium-thick 16″ x 27½″ (40 cm x 70 cm) sheets of silk 'paper', you will need 2 oz (50 g) of silk tops

- Plastic sheet
- Net
- Paint brushes
- Solution
- Washing-up liquid
- Containers
- Mopping-up cloths

Tussah silk tops by 'Treetops Colour Harmonies'

Preparing to make the silk batt — plastic, net and silk tops

First step in preparing the silk tops (see steps 1–5, Preparing the silk tops)

Method

Prepare the work surface

1. Select a working surface—preferably with easy access to water and a sink. Whenever weather permits I prepare my silk 'paper' outside.
2. Lay the sheet of plastic down on your work surface. To obtain a smooth sheet of finished 'paper' ensure the plastic is wrinkle free.
3. Cut four pieces of net approximately 20½" x 32" (52 cm x 82 cm). This will make two sheets of 'paper' as specified above. It is necessary to decide on the size of the 'paper' you wish to make and cut the net accordingly.
4. Remember to cut it 3–4" (7–10 cm) larger all around to accommodate the silk.
5. It is very important that the area where you are working with the silk tops is kept absolutely dry. Water on the silk while you are laying down the batt will make it unmanageable.

Prepare the silk tops

1. Place one piece of net on the plastic sheet. The silk tops will be layered on this.
2. Pull off a manageable length from the top, say 10–15" (26–38 cm). Then, hold the end of the silk in your right hand, gripped between your middle finger and the 'pads' of your hands (the thick part next to your thumb). Hold the long end of the silk top in the same manner with the left hand (reverse these instructions if you are left handed). Your hands should be approximately 5–6" (13–16 cm) apart.
3. Pull gently on the silk tops (no force is required) and a length of silk fibres will come away quite freely. This should be approximately ½ –1" (1–1.5 cm) wide and 4–5" (10–12.5 cm) long.

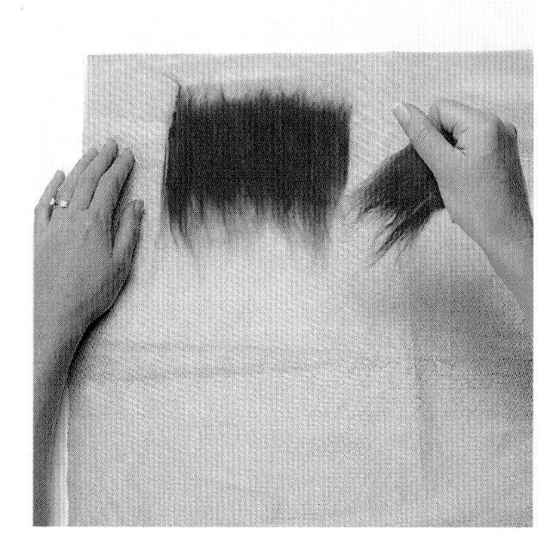

Laying down the silk tops, first layer, row one

4. You may need to give the fibres a few gentle tugs along the length to loosen them up if they have been hand dyed. Strip the top lengthwise as many times as needed to be easily manageable.
5. Should you experience some static electricity while handling the silk, lightly spray the silk tops with an anti-static lingerie spray, which dries in 6–7 minutes. You can then continue to prepare the batt.

Laying down the silk tops

1. It is important that the silk tops are laid down in an orderly manner to ensure that the finished 'paper' has an all-over strength. This especially applies to sheets made for bags, book covers and any other flat items that are to be cut from a single sheet.
2. Begin in the upper left-hand corner of the net, leaving a 2–2¼″ (5–6 cm) border all around. Lay down the silk in a straight line until you have reached the desired size.
3. For the second row you can either work up the net or down from the top left. Either way will do. Continue laying the silk but ensure that the new row overlaps approximately 1⅝ –2¾″ (4–7 cm) on top of the previous row.
4. To put down a second layer, place it at right angles to the first one. Whether you have one, two or three layers will depend on the purpose of the silk 'paper'. This will be a matter of experimentation and how thickly you lay down the silk tops.
5. Follow this method if you are to lay down a third row.
6. The third row will lie at right angles to the second one. In other words, you will have a vertical row, a horizontal row then another vertical row. If you require your paper to be strong in all directions, lay down three thin layers rather than two thick ones.

Completing the first vertical layer
(see steps 1 and 2, Laying down
the silk tops)

Adding the second layer
(see steps 3 and 4, Laying down
the silk tops)

Completing the second layer

Placing the net over the dry batt — ready for' wetting down' and adhesive

7 When making a three-layered sheet, the middle layer is not visible, so you can economise on your favourite colours and use leftovers of another colour.

8 The thickness of the 'paper' is dependent upon the amount of silk you lay in any one place. By experimenting, you will be able to determine the right thickness required for your specific purpose. The highest possible lustre is obtained by keeping all the fibres orderly and parallel to each other.

9 Once you have finished laying down the batt, return the remaining tops to the plastic bag.

10 Using a piece of net the same size as the bottom one, very carefully lay it over the silk. It is difficult to change the position of the net once it has been placed down on the dry silk.

Wetting-out the silk

Silk repels water so it is necessary to help break its surface tension before applying the adhesive. This is done by painting the silk thoroughly on **both sides** with a solution of soapy water.

1 Add the detergent to the bowl—approximately 1 tspn to 10½ fl oz (300 ml) of water. By adding the detergent first, you can more accurately determine how much detergent is in the water and whether you need a richer lather. Agitate the water to mix in the detergent.

2 Using a 2–3″ (5–8 cm) paintbrush, paint the silk thoroughly on both sides. Wipe up excess soapsuds with a sponge or old towel. It is important to work the soapy solution into the silk with strong brush strokes. Do not be concerned that the silk is wet and white from the detergent—this will disappear once the silk is dry. Wet the first side once again—just to ensure you have wet both sides.

Applying the adhesive

1. Prepare the adhesive by following manufacturer's instructions (see Materials and Equipment).
2. Paint on evenly and thoroughly to both sides of the silk, working well into the fibres. As the adhesives are white in colour it is easy to see them on the silk. You can use the same brush that you used for applying the soapy water, just rinse and squeeze out any excess detergent.
3. When painting on the adhesive, do not pour too much solution into your container at any one time. The brush collects surplus detergent from the wetted silk and this dilutes the adhesive.
4. Work the adhesive well into the wet silk. It is important that the silk has been totally wetted down with both water and adhesive. The 'paper' will split into layers if the liquids have not penetrated the silk tops.
5. Move the silk, still sandwiched between the nets, to the drying frame (see Materials and Equipment). To do this, fold the ends of the plastic towards the middle of the net and wet silk to prevent any liquid spilling. Carry the whole lot outside where you can drop the plastic and let the water drain away. Place the wet silk and net onto the drying frame. Do not leave the wet silk to dry on the plastic—it will become shiny from the adhesive remaining on the plastic.
6. Smooth out any wrinkles that may be visible on the net.
7. Wash, or hose down, the plastic to remove the adhesive (you will be able to re-use the plastic several times).
8. Thoroughly wash the brushes and leave them to dry.

Drying the silk and removing the net

1. Always leave the net on until the 'paper' has completely dried. Drying times can vary according to the thickness of the silk 'paper', the adhesive used and the air temperature. Allow up to 24 hours to dry in a cool climate and about 14 hours in a warmer one.
2. Do not dry the silk in direct sunlight because it damages the fibres.
3. When you are sure the 'paper' is completely dry, test a corner to see if the net comes away easily. If the silk is sticking to the net, leave it a little longer and try again. The success of your 'paper' rests on the silk being completely dry before the net is removed.
4. Remove the net from the outer edge first, then from the main body. The net should come away quite freely. When removing the net, always take the net from the silk in the direction that the last layer was laid down.
5. Wash the net and, when dry, remove any excess fibres that have stuck to it. I use a brush for removing lint from clothing. It is possible to use the net several times.
6. Iron the paper. Use a medium heat setting with a press cloth, or sandwich the 'paper' between two sheets of brown paper to smooth out any wrinkles.
7. Remember, you must always press 'paper' you have made using Textile Medium to set the adhesive and make the 'paper' water repellent. This is rather like heat setting textile paints.

Moulding, Sculpting & Texturing

Bowls molded over simple shapes, using a hairdryer to assist the drying process. These are suitable for beginners

By using Acrylic Gloss Medium it is a simple process to make exciting, creative and imaginative pieces. In fact, anything that can be made in paper can be made in silk 'paper'. Look for books on papermaking and adapt the examples for this new medium.

Moulding and Sculpting

By moulding the silk when wet it can be shaped over masks, glass bowls and plastic containers. But beware: do not use your best plastic, as the solution will discolour the plastic. When moulding you can either shape on the inside or the outside of the mould. If using glass, line the container with plastic wrap or aluminium foil to enable you to remove the dry silk without any problems. Ensure that the top of a container is big enough to remove the silk 'paper' when it is dry. If the container has a textured surface you can press the wet silk into the indents. This works better if a thinner batt is used—say one or two layers.

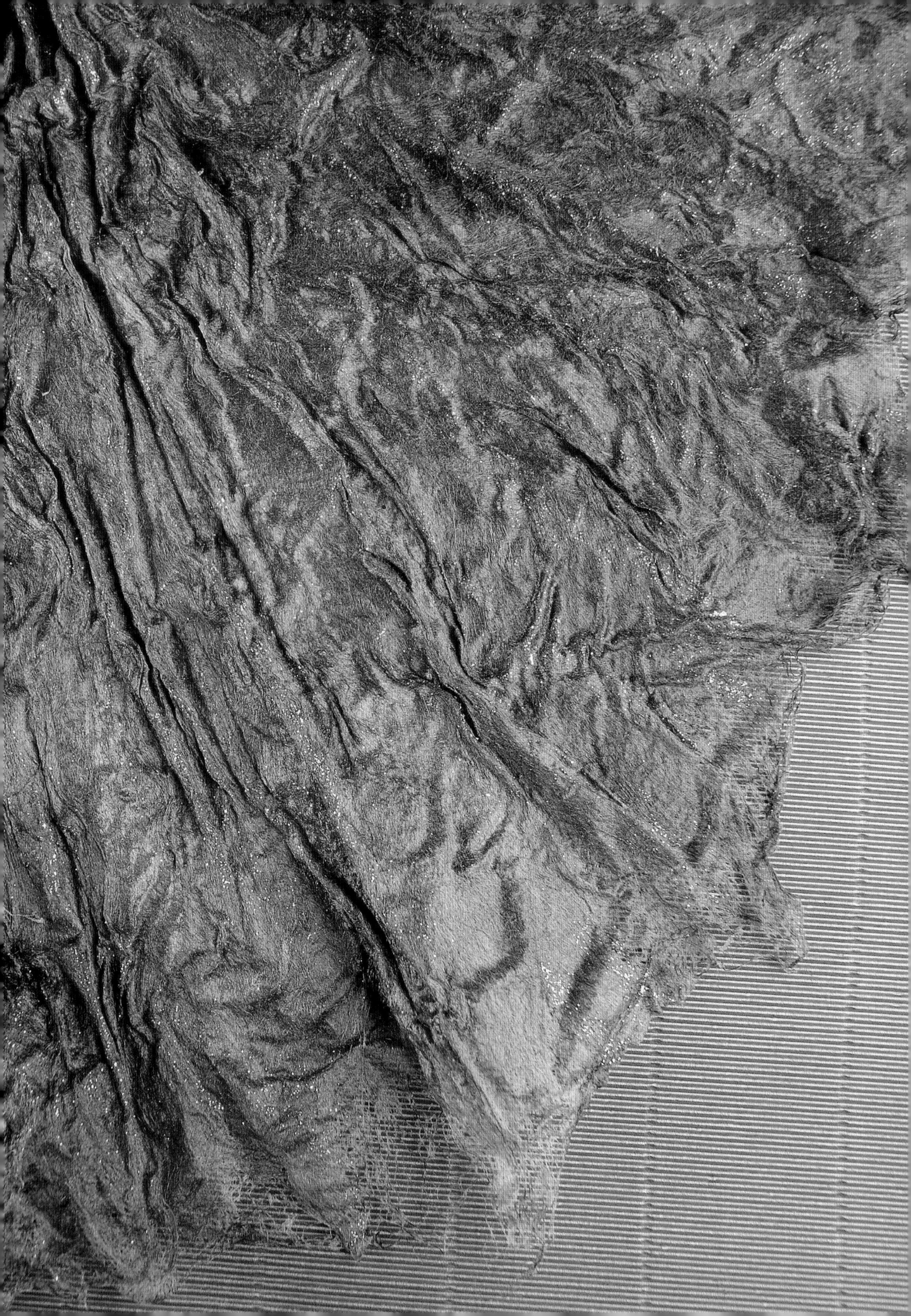

Texturing

You can texture the surface of the 'paper' when the silk is wet. After the adhesive has been applied to both sides of the silk, remove the top layer of net and manipulate the surface of the wet silk with your fingers to make raised lines and indentations. Carefully lift the silk—still with the bottom layer of net—to a drying frame, and make any adjustments to the shaping before leaving the silk to dry. You can continue changing the surface until the 'paper' becomes too dry to manipulate. It can take up to 18 hours or more to dry, depending on the thickness and size of the piece. This technique is best suited to the Acrylic Gloss Medium.

Should you wish to use the textured piece as a three dimensional motif, the drying process can be accelerated by using a hairdryer. Using a hairdryer will make the work more rigid than if it has been left to dry naturally.

The wet silk has been textured by hand before being left to dry. Once dry the surface has been highlighted with oil paintstiks

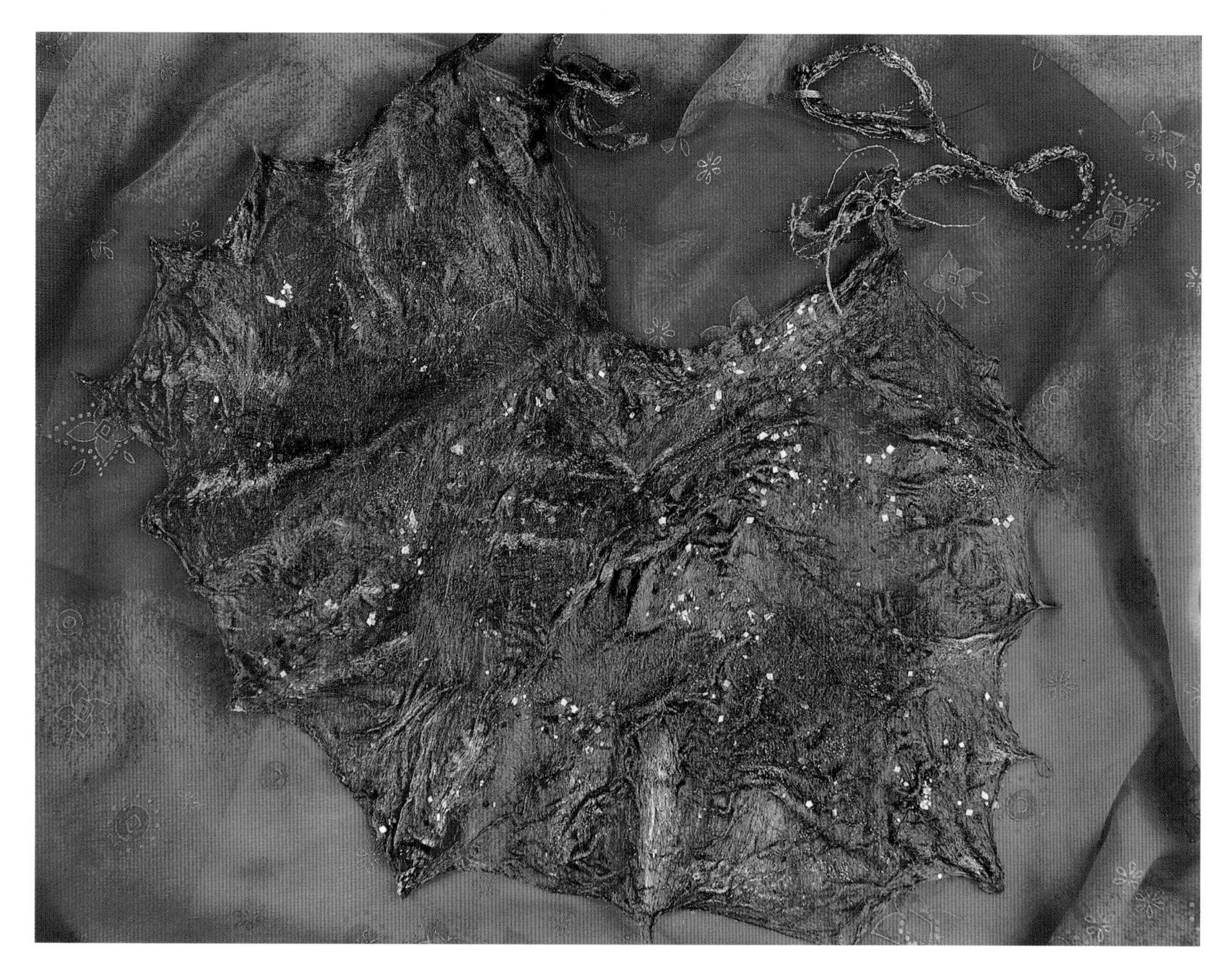

This collar combines both open work—lace and inlaying of glitter on the surface

Making a lace-like surface

It is possible to produce a gossamer-like appearance when the silk is in the 'wet' stage prior to drying. Remove the net from both sides of the wet silk—the batt is strong at this stage but take care just the same. Place the wet silk on a flat surface. Gently pull the fibres apart so that holes appear with thin strands of silk fibres still remaining across the holes. This pulling can be worked all over the wet silk or in selected areas. Leave the silk to dry on a frame. With this technique it is easier to take the frame to the silk and carefully lift it on to the frame to dry.

This technique is most effective when used with a transparent fabric placed behind the dry silk 'paper'. Experiment with organza, chiffon or even dyed muslin. All are light and well suited for this purpose. This technique can be a little difficult to master but the end results will be most rewarding.

Inlaying

Adding threads to the surface of the 'paper' is done after you have laid down the last layer of silk fibres, and before the second sheet of net is placed on top of the dry silk. Use threads (plain and metallic) decorative wools, small pieces of fabric, or glitter pieces that will add interest to the surface without detracting from the silk.

Carefully lay the threads on the dry silk tops—not too thickly or the beauty of the silk will be lost. Pull away a delicate web of silk tops and lay them on top of the threads. Use just enough silk to contain the threads on the surface. Taking care not to disturb the surface threads, carefully place the net on top of the dry silk and wet down with the detergent, followed by the adhesive. When the silk has dried and the net has been removed, the surface threads will be embossed on the finished 'paper'.

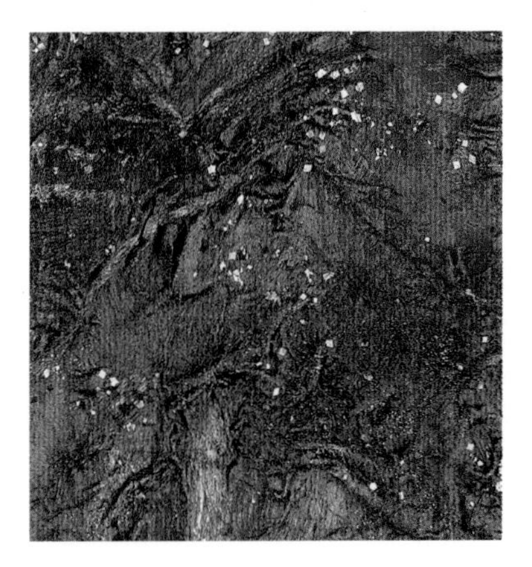

Embellishing Silk 'Paper'

ABOVE: Theatre Purse—beaded fringe, twin needling, machined cord. 6½" x 7½" (17 cm x 19 cm)

OPPOSITE: Triptych—Byzantine inspired. Simulated filigree using fine gold metallic threads. Appliqué, cords and semi-precious stones. Triptych folds into one unit. All over 15¾" x 7" (40 cm x 18 cm)

Design and Inspiration

Silk 'paper' is easy to cut and it stitches well by hand or machine. As the surface is so lustrous, it is possible to over-embellish it and lose some of the beauty of the silken surface. Although I enjoy hand embroidery, my chosen tool for decorating the 'paper' is the sewing machine.

Toning colours, using fine machine embroidery threads in plain and metallic, small pieces of applied fabrics and touches of metallic fabric paints, will enrich your 'paper'. Use these to create a myriad of exotic pieces that have no purpose other than that they can be a talking point on your coffee table.

You can manipulate and mould the 'paper' when wet to create unusual and interesting forms by using the Acrylic Gloss Medium. If you do not like the finished form, simply wet down the shape and recreate a new one.

Make a simple box using a small amount of machining, but add highlights with beads—these really make the 'paper' sing.

Silk 'paper' quilts beautifully. Using the positive/negative method will produce some interesting results. When using a grid design the surface will take on a textured appearance.

Make original bag 'flaps' by pleating the paper to create your own designer fronts and bag shapes.

TOP: 'Cocktails'. Machine couched decorative cords, appliquéd brocade, long silk beaded tassel

ABOVE: 'Peacock' hat. Machine stitching on crown and brim. Emerald feather trim, purple silk lining

RIGHT: 'Woodland'. Full length kimono. Manipulated and pulled fibres for a lace-like surface. Highlighted with metallic paintstiks. Collar is detachable

It is quite simple to stencil, paint or spray paint on to the silk, as it takes paint well and dries quickly. Using thick textile paints and a brush or roller, put your individual mark on the lustrous silk, taking care not to obscure too much of its beauty.

'Bird of Paradise' cape. Single batt of 'paper'. Manipulated and pulled fibres for a lace-like surface

Wearable art is yet another area in which you can design highly individual work. Hats, capes—even full length garments are possible—waistcoats, panels sewn into silk fabric, felt garments, even panels sewn on to wool fabric all lend themselves to the beauty of silk 'paper'.

Silk 'paper' is incredibly user friendly. Many of its versatile qualities are yet to be discovered. Once you feel comfortable working with the 'paper', you can begin to experiment and use it in your own way. Not only will you be making your own substrate but you will be creating a totally individual piece of work.

Inspiration can be found all around us. Nature is a great source: flowers, plants, landscapes, fungi, animals and birds. Architecture, mosaics, symbolism, pre-historic artifacts and Celtic art also inspire designs. Consider the wonderful flowing lines of the Art Nouveau period and compare them with the geometric Art Deco style.

There are ethnic styles—Indian, Egyptian and Byzantine—which have all had a great influence on my work. These three cultures are so rich in colour and decorative art that they lend themselves well to silk 'paper'. I never tire of researching and sketching from the reference books that I have on these cultures.

OPPOSITE & ABOVE: 'Medieval Magic'. A reliquary inspired by the Byzantine period. Richly embroidered using gold threads, cords, beads, pearls and semi-precious stones. The lid lifts off to reveal a red silk lining. 7½" x 13" (19 cm diameter x 33 cm high)

Don't forget exhibitions. They do not necessarily need to be of textiles. Take the opportunity to view ceramics, paintings and jewellery—they all abound with designs and ideas that can be translated into textile art.

Being able to see design is one thing, interpreting what you see is another. Collect ideas. Keep them in sketchbooks and scrapbooks, together with photos, fabric samples, cuttings and colour combinations that have excited you. Over time, you will have an extensive reference 'library' from which to draw ideas.

Spend time making samples, as they are the best and most lasting record from which you can recreate a technique that you have found exciting. Record the whole process, the threads, stitches and techniques used for working your sample, as we do not always remember the details afterwards.

When you see fabrics and threads that catch your eye, buy them (if possible). You are surely going to want to use them some time and wish that you had purchased them. Keep a register of suppliers. Get mail order catalogues and ask fellow embroiderers to share their suppliers in exchange for some of yours!

Being able to 'see' design everywhere you look is an acquired skill, which may take some time to cultivate.

Suggested Equipment & Materials

- A sewing machine in good working order, extension lead, manual and accessory box
- Machine needles: sizes 10–12 (70–80)
- Scissors—small embroidery scissors with good points, shears and paper scissors
- Rotary cutter or craft knife
- Cutting board
- A beading needle
- A tape measure
- Sharp pointed long pins
- Fabric paints: including gold, copper and silver paints and metallic powders
- Brushes for use with fabric paints
- Containers for washing brushes
- Rags for cleaning brushes and mopping up
- If you wish to experiment with water soluble fabric, you will need a machine embroidery frame for making motifs to apply to the silk 'paper'
- Jewellery findings, if you fancy making necklaces, earrings and brooches
- Stiff card for stencils and tassel making
- Tracing paper or non-stick baking paper

- Notebooks and sketch pads for your ideas and designs
- Selection of machine embroidery threads, plain and metallic
- Beads and sequins
- Narrow silk or rayon ribbon, decorative wools, DMC type cottons, textured and metallic cords—all useful for couching and as straps for bags
- Fabrics: glitz fabric, nets, tulle, organza, satin ribbon, embroidery floss, glitzy yarns, metallic fabrics and/or silk fabric
- Light-weight batting for quilting
- Velcro for bag closures

Tools I just can't do without!

- Small tweezers
- Thread racks —I select the colours and types of threads to be used on a particular project and keep them handy on the racks.
- At least two tape measures
- Metal sewing/knitting gauge
- 'Innovations' needle release pad; when machining silk 'paper' the needle collects dried solution and needs to be cleaned regularly so machining through these pads removes the solution—pads are available at machine shops
- Pins and scissors wherever I am working
- Dressmaker's chalk and a white pencil
- The open embroidery foot for my sewing machine

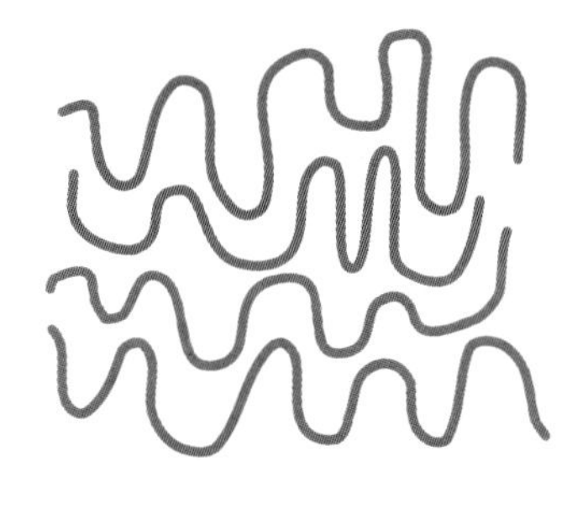

Some suggested stitch patterns for mark making

Transferring Designs and Mark Making

See diagram 'Suggested stitch patterns for mark making'. Mark making on silk 'paper' is more restricted than on conventional fabric. The surface of the 'paper' is like paper and felt so the methods that work for fabrics are not so easy to implement. The following methods give ample 'marks' to enable a design to be visible on the 'paper'.

- Marking pens, the sort that fade away, are suitable for light coloured 'paper' but they are difficult to distinguish on darker 'paper'.
- A well-sharpened white pencil works well, as does a piece of white soap with a carved point. Both of these will fade away.
- Dressmaker's chalk is another alternative.
- The method I use most frequently for marking out more complicated designs is the 'trace and stitch' method. Trace the design on to tracing or non-stick baking paper. I prefer the latter as it is much stronger and more transparent. Tack the design to the work and if you feel confident using the machine, stitch around the design using a long stitch or tacking stitch. Using toning thread makes it a little harder to see, but the stitches are less obvious on the background. If you prefer, you can stitch the design by hand. When you have completed the tacking, carefully tear the tracing paper away. A pair of tweezers can be helpful for removing any stubborn pieces of tracing paper.

Decorative Techniques

Threads and stitching

Machine embroidery threads are much finer than conventional sewing threads, and they suit the lustrous surface of the silk 'paper'. There are many brands on the market and you will probably have your favourite ones. By incorporating plain, variegated and metallic threads, you can embellish the surface with stitching alone.

Use a size 10 or 12 (70 or 80) needle. A thicker needle will leave marks in the silk 'paper'. However, you can use a thicker needle and lace fine threads through the holes to give texture to surface. If you are using metallic threads use a metafil or top stitching needle.

Twin needles are most effective on silk 'paper'. Using a plain and a metallic thread together will add further richness to the surface.

I mostly use straight stitch with either the open embroidery or darning foot. The open foot gives very good visibility and is excellent for couching wools, fancy cords and braids. When using straight stitch, lengthen the stitch a little (machines vary, so experiment with the stitch length). Remember to loosen the top tension to prevent the machine embroidery threads from breaking.

Free machine embroidery requires no frame because of the body in the silk 'paper'. It is difficult to frame the 'paper' and the frame will mark the 'paper'.

A selection of threads, cords, satins, silks and wools that can be used to embellish silk 'paper'

ABOVE & OPPOSITE: 'Finished—but Unfinished'. Design taken from the inserts sewn into the front of long shifts worn by women in Kutch and other remote parts of India 18½" x 19" (38 cm x 48 cm)

Flat applique

I like to create a jewel-like effect on my 'paper' using a technique I call Mosaic Applique. Quite simply, cut tiny pieces of rich fabrics—satin, silk and metallic—and, using double-sided webbing, apply the 'mosaic' pieces to the 'paper'. Double-sided fusible webbing comes on a transparent backing paper and is known as Vliesofix and Wonder Under. This fine sticky web is ideal for applique. Select your fabric to be applied and iron the sticky side to the back of the fabric. Draw your shapes onto the paper backing or free cut the shapes to be applied.

Before ironing the applied shapes, heat test them for temperature. Remove the transparent backing paper and place baking paper on top of the fabric to be applied. This will protect the iron from picking up any of the fusible webbing. With a moderately hot iron, adhere the shapes to the background. The baking paper should protect any fabric that is unable to withstand too much heat. The web prevents the fabric pieces from fraying, and all that is required to contain the fabric is two to three rows of straight stitching, either with the presser or the darning foot.

With my interest in Indian embroidery and the rich colours that are used, I have a never-ending source of inspiration for design and colour.

ABOVE: Vessel—'Will not hold Water'. A stencilled design from an Indian monument cut as a continuous length and sewn to form a cylindrical shape 4¾" x 9 " (12 cm x 23 cm)

Reverse applique

Reverse applique is also a suitable technique to use with silk 'paper'. In this method, two or more layers of fabric are placed one over the other, and stitched at the back of the work. Each layer is cut away from the top of the work in part, to reveal the fabric below. As silk 'paper' does not fray, it is an ideal substrate to use for this technique. I have used this technique in both 'Finished—but Unfinished' (page 52) and 'Luxor' (page 56).

Cutwork works well on silk 'paper' because it does not fray. All that is needed is two or three rows of stitching to contain the cut edge. (see 'Luxor' page 56)

Quilting

Silk 'paper' lends itself very well to quilting because of the rich lustre of the silk. When preparing your paper for quilting you can use either two sheets of one-layered 'paper' with a light-weight wool batting sandwiched in between, or a two-layered sheet of 'paper' with batting and muslin or light-weight calico on the back.

For straight lines use the open embroidery foot—this foot gives very good visibility when sewing. For intricate or curving designs that call for free machining, use the darning or quilting foot.

If you are making a wall hanging, the filmy edges of the silk 'paper' can become an integral part of the piece. Prepare the silk 'paper' to the size you want the finished piece. With a single-layer batt there will only be two sides with a feathery edge, so your second piece, for the back, will be turned at right angles to the first layer. This will give four sides with a feathery edge.

If you are using a design, transfer it to the top layer of 'paper'. Tack the wool batting to the back of the top layer of 'paper'. As this batting does not appear to catch on the feed plate when stitching, it is not necessary to use the backing 'paper' at this stage. It is only after you have done most of the stitching that you add the backing.

Complete sewing the design with the backing 'paper' behind the work. Sew the three layers together with enough stitching to secure the backing. This gives a neat finish to the back of the work. See 'Pharaoh's Gold', also 'Finished—but Unfinished' (page 52) and 'Luxor' (page 56).

BELOW: 'Pharaohs Gold'—Egyptian inspired, machine quilted with appliqued and beaded motif 15¾" x 19½" (40 cm x 50 cm)

Detail—'Luxor' shows machine quilting, and cut back with a bronze metallic fabric underneath

Metallic powders

When used in very small quantities, these can be most effective for highlighting work. The powders come in silver, gold, bronze, copper and are available from craft supply shops. Using a wooden toothpick and a surface (such as a small plastic lid that can be disposed of) mix a tiny quantity of powder with either Ormaline medium or PVA glue to make a thick paste. Use the toothpick to apply the paste to small areas of the work. Avoid using a paint brush, as the glue can prove impossible to remove. Please take care when mixing these powders—they are toxic. Always wear a mask to avoid inhaling any particles, and wash your hands afterwards. Clean up any spills with an old damp cloth—never brush away the dry powder.

'Luxor'—wall hanging Egyptian inspired. Machine quilting, cut back surface shows metallic fabric underneath. Top flap lifts to reveal rich beading. Feathery edges are an integral part of the design. A tasselled silk cord is used to hang the work 17" x 11½" (30 cm x 44 cm)

Textile paints

The surface of silk 'paper' is similar to paper and is receptive to paints. The paint should be thick so that it does not sink into the surface of the 'paper'. Apply by brush, roller, sponge, block stamp or found objects. Paints go on very easily but it is difficult to write on the surface. Experiment with fabric paints, not forgetting that gold will enrich the surface of the 'paper'. Paints can be applied to silk 'paper' made either with Acrylic Gloss or Textile Medium.

Spray paint

Spray paint gives excellent results and can either be used alone or with a stencil. I use domestic spray paint—gold and silver—from the hardware shop.

Tassels

Made by hand or machine, tassels will add further interest to your work. Tassels made on the machine using machine embroidery threads look very delicate and make an elegant accessory for a bag or box. Use fine or thick threads, ribbons, cords, wool, silk, DMC type cottons, space-dyed rayon, embroidery floss, even off-cut discarded threads from the workroom floor. The choice is never ending. Try torn thin strips of fabric (satin, silk and metallic), shells, coins, feathers, even tiny buttons can be sewn on to your tassels. Tassels are used for celebration and joy by many cultures around the world.

Tassels can be made by hand or on the machine, using plain and metallic threads

OPPOSITE: 'Elephants'—hexagonal box. Beaded tassels, appliqued silk fabrics, elephants printed with gold textile paints, metallic cords and threads. Lined with purple silk 8½" x 9½" (22 cm x 24 cm)

Beads

Start a collection of beads of all colours, shapes and sizes. There are glass beads—also called seed beads—that are tiny and round and come in a wide choice of colours. These are usually sold by weight, as they are so small. Bugle beads are long, tube-shaped beads with a smooth round surface. The bigger bugle beads can be quite heavy, so use a strong thread if sewing with them.

Sequins and shisha add glitter and shine to work. Shisha are very small pieces of mirror glass usually cut into rounds, squares or rectangles. These are used extensively in Indian embroidery, particularly that which comes from Rajasthan and Gujarat. Make your own beads from rolled up strips of painted paper. Seek out metal, wooden and any unusual beads.

ABOVE AND RIGHT: A richly beaded tassel highlights this container

Three-dimensional motifs

Using water-soluble fabric, construct motifs to complement, or contrast with, the silk 'paper'. Frame the water-soluble fabric (I use the cold water variety of water soluble fabric). Using machine embroidery threads, together with snippets of rich fabrics, create one or more motifs with the sewing machine. Cut around the motif leaving just a fraction of water-soluble fabric. Hold it under the cold tap for a minute or two, but do not completely wash away all the soluble fabric.

Pin the motif to a soft pin board and dry it with a hairdryer. You can form the motif with your fingers as it dries. The soluble fabric remaining in the motif will make it firm, especially when dried quickly.

Artists paintstiks

Paintstiks, known as 'Markal Stiks', are sticks of oil paint that can be used on paper or fabric, and they are obtainable from art and craft shops. They work extremely well on silk 'paper' and are most effective when used to highlight 'paper' that has been sculptured and textured (see Moulding, Sculpturing and Texturing).

There is a very extensive range of plain, iridescent, glitter and metallic colours. Because they are shaped like a fat crayon, it is easy to control the placement of colour on your work. Leave the paint to dry for at least 24 hours then iron the work using brown paper, which will pick up any residue of oil paint. These are colour fast and dry-cleanable.

Tips & Troubleshooting

Pinning and Cutting

You can't pin dry silk 'paper' as you would conventional fabric. When cutting out a pattern, place the silk 'paper' on a firm padded surface, like an ironing board. Push the pin halfway into the 'paper' with the point of the pin towards the centre of the work. With the point towards the centre you are less likely to catch the scissors on the pins. This method will hold the 'paper' firmly enough for cutting out the pattern.

Curved Surfaces

Any curved surface, such as a curved lid, should be made using Textile Medium. The body of the container should be made in Acrylic Gloss to make it rigid. Because Textile Medium has a softer finish than Acrylic Gloss it is easier to manipulate the 'paper' made using this medium.

Pattern Cutting

If you wish to control the colour placement on 'paper' that has more than one colour, make the pattern in transparent paper. If you have a sheet of silk 'paper' with more than one colour, try cutting out the pattern placed on the diagonal. The colours in the silk 'paper' will be distributed in a more interesting way. By using transparent paper for the pattern it will be quite easy to manouvre the colours around the shape of the pattern.

Cutting

Use sharp scissors with good points. Alternatively, a rotary cutter or craft knife used with a cutting board will give a straight, smooth line. As the 'paper' has no grain, it can be cut in any direction, making it very economical to use.

Unpicking stitches

Holes can be smoothed out by ironing or rubbing them gently with your fingernail.

Masking Tape

You must take great care when using masking tape. If you use it at all, be very careful when lifting it from the 'paper', as some of the surface fibres will lift away with the tape.

Projects

Bowls & Containers

It is a simple process to produce a bowl or container by using a simple shape or form. Old plastic food containers—takeaway ones—are good to begin with. It is not necessary for the container to be exactly the shape of the finished piece you have in mind. This is where your imagination comes into its own, and you will soon be creating unusual shapes from everyday forms.

OPPOSITE & ABOVE: 'Tassels and Trims' Boxes with removable lids. Tassels and free machine embroidery make the red box 'sing'. The blue box is embellished with motifs constructed from calico that has been dyed and painted, then stitched with tiny pieces of fabric and threads 4" x 4" (10 cm x 10 cm)

- Select a cheap plastic container—not too big—a cereal bowl from a chain store will do. Run a tape measure from the rim of the bowl down the inside to the bottom of the bowl, then up to the rim on the opposite side of bowl. This will tell you how big your piece of 'paper' will need to be. Using Acrylic Gloss Medium, prepare the silk batt. To get an idea of the size for the batt, cut a paper pattern using the measurement you have taken and place it under the plastic before laying down the net and silk. You can work around this pattern. Remember that the finished 'paper' will always be a little bigger than the dry batt.
- Wet the silk with water and adhesive then remove both layers of net. At this stage the silk will have bonded well and will be quite strong. Prepare a thick pad of newspapers and move the work onto it. Have a bucket of water handy to wash the brushes, plastic, and net in.
- Drape the wet silk over the bowl or container you have chosen as a mould. Using a hairdryer, gently mould the wet silk into shape. Don't worry about it not being exactly the same as the mould—this is your individual work and you will find yourself sculpting the 'paper' into an original form. The 'paper' will be

ABOVE: Vessel—'Will not hold Water'. A stencilled design from an Indian monument cut as a continuous length and sewn to form a cylindrical shape 4¾" x 9 " (12 cm x 23 cm)

ABOVE RIGHT: Bowls molded over simple shapes, using a hairdryer to assist the drying process. These are suitable for beginners

thicker in the centre of the mould, so that section will take longer to dry.

- The edges will have a 'wispy' appearance. Sculpt them around your fingers or roll them around a pencil. At this stage, you may think of other ways to shape the edges. When the bowl is beginning to feel dry (this may take an hour or more) you can leave the 'paper,' returning to complete the drying and sculpting process before it has dried completely.
- Once the 'paper' has dried, it can be effective to draw or 'smudge' on the surface of the 'paper'. Using an oil paintstik, gently brush the top of the raised surface to highlight the texture. You can also lightly sponge the surface with textile paints.

Now, if for any reason you are not happy with the finished result do not worry. Just wet down the shape with a little water (not too much), add more Acrylic Gloss, and reshape!

Masks

'Oberons Mask'—free machine embroidery, applied metallic fabrics and threads 14" x 25" (35 cm x 65 cm)

If you enjoy the challenge of designing and are interested in theatrical costumes, then mask making will excite you. Look for books that depict ethnic masks—Egyptian, African, Indian, Venetian and Balinese—to help you to get started in designing your own. Draw up motifs and border designs, also colour combinations—not forgetting the embellishment.

Materials

- A simple 'party shop' mask to use as a guide—do not be concerned if you are unable to find one that is exactly the shape you wish to make
- Colourful threads, metallic threads, sequin waste or any other embellishments
- Silk tops

Method

1. To establish the finished size and the amount of 'paper' you will require, measure from side to side, across the nose allowing extra width for the nose. This will give you the width of the face and also allow for the eye cavities.
2. Determine how far you would like the mask to extend either side of the face, above the forehead and below the chin. These measurements are a rough guide as to the size of 'paper' you will need.
3. Once you have an idea of how your mask might look, make the 'paper' using Acrylic Gloss Medium. For added strength, make a three-layered batt.
4. At this stage you can scatter glitter or threads on the surface (see Embellishing Silk 'Paper'). When the 'paper' has dried it is time to begin the embellishing. At this stage you will have a flat dry sheet of 'paper'. Place the mask beneath the sheet of 'paper' and roughly establish where the nose and eye sockets might be. Mark with chalk to give a guide and cut out holes for the eyes. Remember to leave adequate space between the eyes for the bridge of the nose.

OPPOSITE & BELOW: 'Charlston'—mask. Couched metallic threads, free machine, beaded silk tassel. Headpiece and mask can be worn as one, or as two separate items

'Butterfly'— mask. Free machine embroidery, applique, sequin waste, metallic threads, cords and sequinned net

5. Work the surface with stitching, applique, couching or free machining, or throw on some fabric paints, sequins or sequin waste!
6. When you have finished embellishing the flat mask, make a pad from newspapers and wet down the mask, stitching and all.
7. Brush on some detergent (not too much) and more Acrylic Gloss Medium.
8. When the 'paper' is wet (but not too wet) lift it onto the mask form and begin to shape it with your hands. Mould a bump for the nose, working the wet 'paper' around the nose on the mask form.

'Carnivale'— mask. Gold braids, sequinned net, woven metallic fabrics, sequinn waste

9 Use a hairdryer as you go. It will take some time to dry completely but, once the actual form becomes visible and the 'paper' is reasonably dry, you can leave it and return to complete the drying later on.

10 If you wish to wear the mask, you need to sew a small square of silk 'paper' to the back of the mask on the outside of the eye holes to reinforce it before sewing on thin metallic ribbons or strips of fabric for tying the mask around the head.

A Simple Neck Purse

OPPOSITE & ABOVE: A selection of Neck Purses featuring suggested designs for flaps and openings

With a single thread in the needle and using the line of the flap as a guide, I stitched free flowing lines over the front, flap and back. Two purple metallic machine embroidery threads were then used in the needle to stitch over selected lines on the background. By using two threads in the needle, a corded effect was obtained.

You can add extra interest to your purse by attaching tassels to either side of the top, or to the centre of the flap.

Materials

- A sheet of silk 'paper' approximately 14″ x 16″ (35 cm x 40 cm) made with textile medium—three thin layers are best for this project ('Paper' to be pressed before use)
- Vilene or heavy paper for pattern
- Pencils, or black felt pen, for pattern
- Scissors for cutting paper
- Machine embroidery threads, plain and metallic
- A selection of cords, wools and thick threads for the neck cord—the thickness of the cord/ribbons/threads will determine how many lengths you need but the neck cord should not be too heavy
- Usual sewing materials
- Sewing machine and open embroidery foot or presser foot
- A darning foot for any free machine work
- Velcro, approximately 2″ (5 cm) for closure

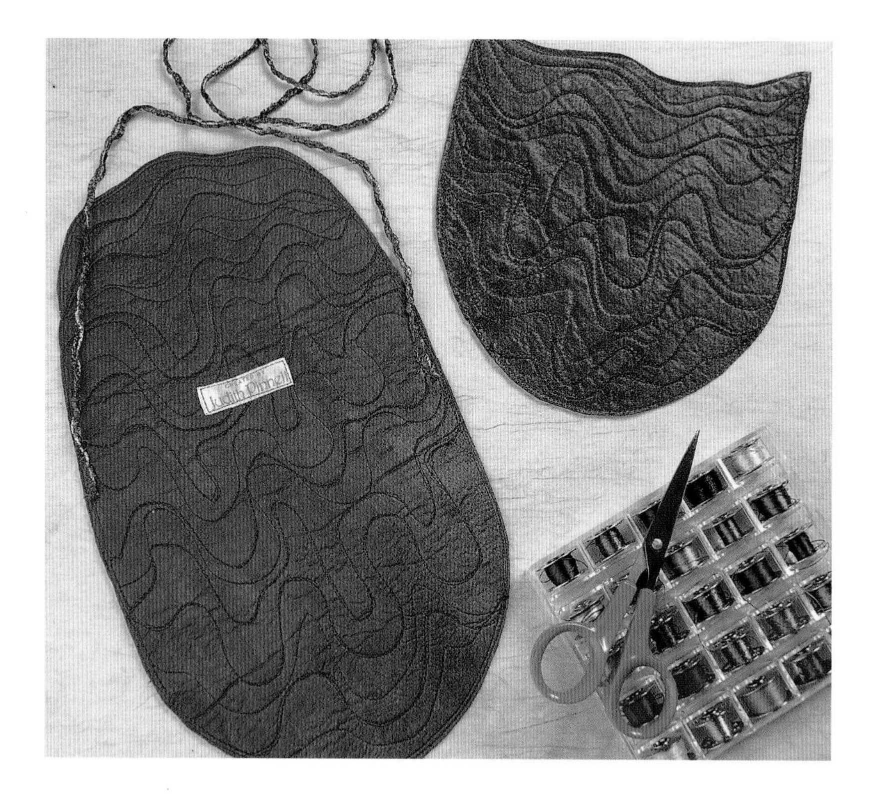

Neck purse in construction—shows placement for neck cord, label, and machine stitching

Method

1. Draw up the pattern, marking in details as shown (see pattern).
2. Pin the pattern to the silk 'paper'.
3. Cut out the pieces using sharp scissors.
4. Select your machine embroidery threads to use on the top and in the bobbin. Remember to slightly loosen the top thread tension and lengthen the stitch when using machine embroidery threads. Experiment with some silk 'paper before starting to stitch.
5. Stitch close to the outer edge, around the front and back of the purse, to stabilise the edges of the 'paper'.
6. Fold and press the front flap as shown on the pattern.
7. Open out the pressed flap and proceed to work your decorative stitching. Having marked the front flap, you will be able to decide whether you wish to do extra stitching to emphasise that area, or keep the stitching the same all over.

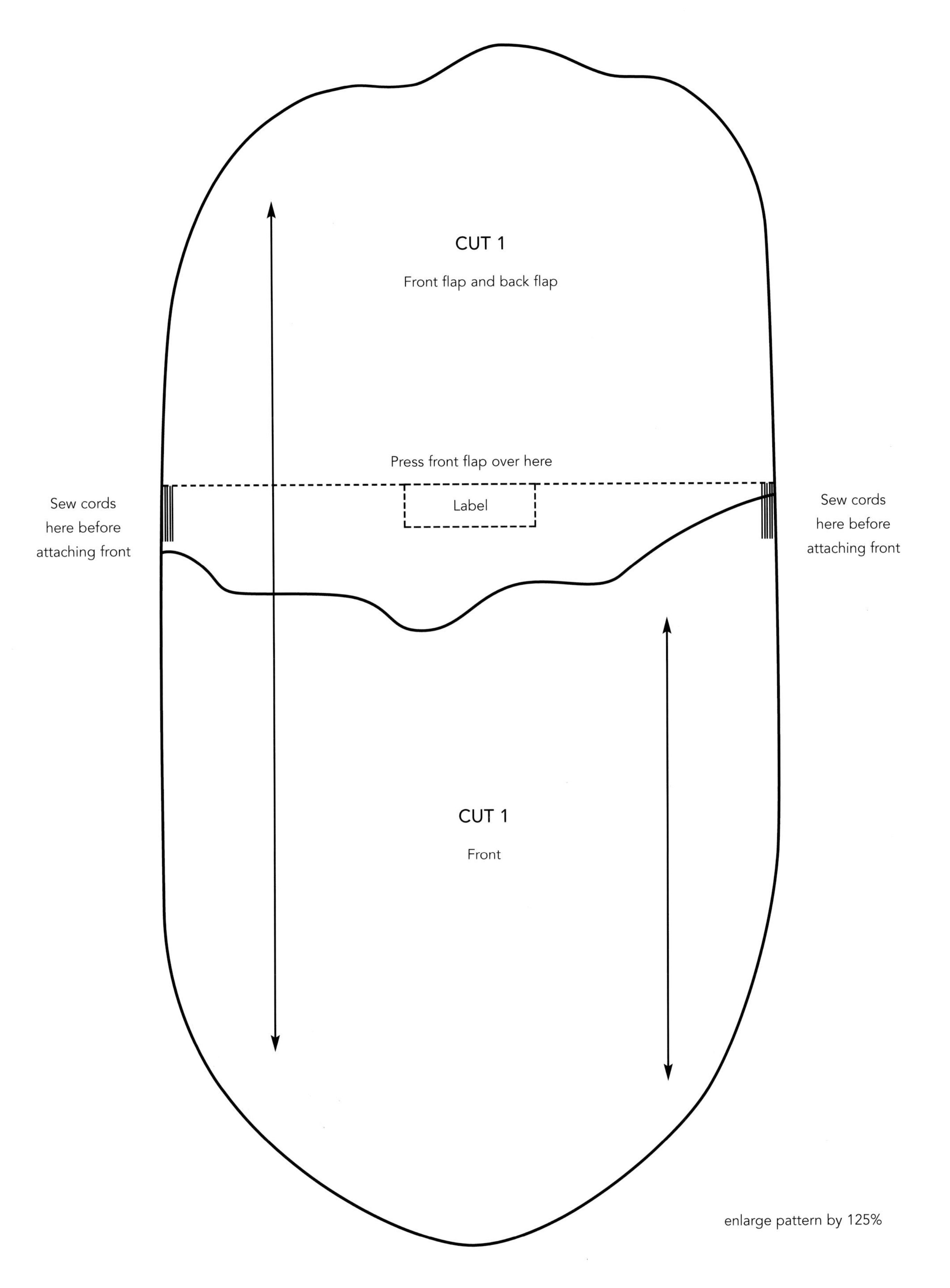

enlarge pattern by 125%

To make the neck cord

1. Select four or five lengths of cord, ribbons or threads (such as Twilley's Goldfinger). You can cut off the lengths before stitching or after you have sewn the neck cord.
2. Lay the threads close together, blending the colours and textures.
3. Set the sewing machine to running stitch (no. 3 on the Bernina). Use machine embroidery threads—plain or metallic (a combination of metallic thread on the top and a plain in the bobbin can be effective).
4. The stitch width will automatically be at the widest setting when using the running stitch. Make the stitch length a little longer so that the stitching does not cover too much of the cords/ribbons/threads. Test the stitch before starting to sew the neck cord.
5. Pull out about 6″ (15 cm) of machine threads. Place the cords/ribbons/threads together beneath the machine foot, holding them taut. Sew along the cords/ribbons/threads, pulling the stitched end (at the back of the machine) gently away from you while, at the same time, steadying the unstitched cords at the front. You can stitch them flat or gently twist as you sew.
6. When you have stitched approximately 43″ (108 cm), or your required length, cut the machine threads and the cords/ribbons/threads.
7. The running stitch will secure the threads but, if you want to be sure, you can sew a couple of reverse stitches. This makes a very firm neck cord. Return the machine to straight stitch.
8. If you have a label, sew this on now while the purse is still out flat (see placement on pattern page 77).

Attaching the neck cord

1 Stitch the cord approximately 1" (2.5 cm) down on the inside of the back as shown on the pattern.
2 Sew close to the edge, making sure that the ends of the cord have all been caught in the stitching, but are not protruding from the side of the purse.
3 Sew up and down three or four times using a straight stitch to secure the cord.
4 Trim away any excess threads inside the purse.

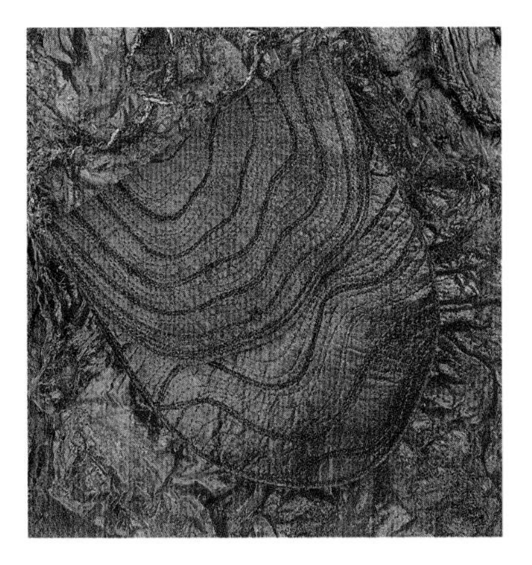

Completed Neck purse. The free machine stitching is influenced by the line of the flap

Stitching on the Velcro fastening

1 Cut a small piece of Velcro, about 5/8" (1.5 cm) in diameter (black or white depending on the colour of the purse).
2 Round off the corners to make an oval shape.
3 Match the front of the purse to the back as if preparing to sew them together. Mark where the Velcro will go by pushing a pin through the flap to the front of the purse. Mark the front with a second pin.
4 Stitch one piece of Velcro inside the flap where marked, and one piece to the outside of the front where marked.

Front to back

1 Pin the front to the back and stitch together.
2 Stitch three or four stitches along the top edge of the purse before stitching down the sides. This strengthens the sides of the top opening.

Small Box with Flap Lid

I used scraps of gold kid, silk, metallic fabric and satin to make the tiny coloured rectangles on the lid of this box. Reverse applique was worked on the lid using a square of black silk 'paper' and a square of gold kid. Great extravagance!

The 'topknot' was made from six small machine-made tassels turned upside down and attached with a narrow strip of gold kid stitched around the heads of the tassels. The tassels were sewn on by hand to the centre of the lid after the box was assembled.

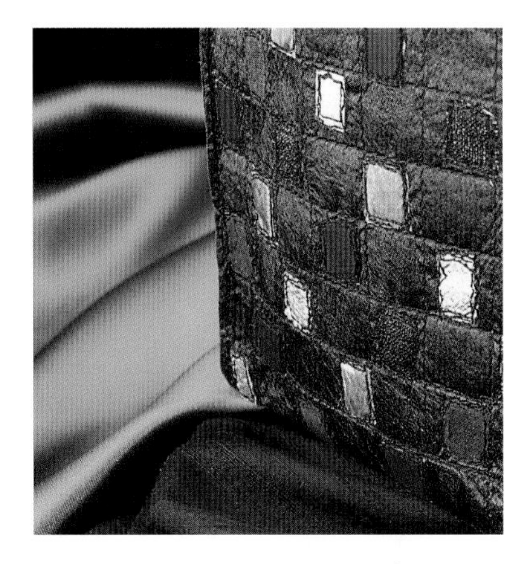

OPPOSITE & ABOVE: Box—embellished with tiny pieces of applied satin and gold kid. The lid is part of the body of the box and has a reverse applique motif of gold kid, silk paper and threads 4″ x 4″ (10 cm x 10 cm)

Materials

- Sheet of silk 'paper' made using Acrylic Gloss Medium, measuring at least 20″ x 16″ (50 cm x 40 cm)—three thin layers work best for this project
- Stiff paper, at least 20″ x 16″ (50 cm x 40 cm) for pattern
- Pencils, ruler, set square (for preparing the pattern)
- Sharp scissors
- Machine embroidery threads (plain and metallic)
- Scraps of 'glitz' fabrics (silk, satin) of your choice, to embellish the box
- Double-sided web (Vliesofix) for applying small pieces of fabric
- Usual sewing materials
- Sewing machine, open embroidery foot if you have one, darning foot for any free machining

Method

1. Draw up the Pattern, marking in the details.
2. The pattern is half the finished size, which will be 4″ (10 cm) on all sides.
3. Pin pattern to the silk 'paper' and, using sharp scissors, cut out the box.
4. Thread the machine with machine embroidery thread on top and in the bobbin. Use a size 10 or 12 (70–80 cm) needle. Slightly loosen the upper tension and lengthen the sewing stitch a little. Experiment with some silk 'paper' to determine the most suitable stitch length and how much of the upper thread tension to release.
5. With either the presser or open embroidery foot (I prefer the latter), sew twice around the outer edge of the box shape as close to the edge as you can, to secure the edges and prevent the 'paper' from splitting.
6. Press sides 1 to 4 and the lid of the box towards the base along the fold lines, as shown on the pattern. This enables you to embellish the sections of the box you would like to be prominent.

Because the silk 'paper' is stiff, it is not necessary to use an embroidery frame. You can easily work free stitching without framing the work. Use the machine tray to stabilise the work.

Embellishing the box

1. Try any of the following techniques:
   - Applique small pieces of fabric for a mosaic effect, using double-sided webbing to adhere the pieces ready for stitching. (See Embellishing Silk 'Paper')
   - Couch rich cords, ribbons or braids.

SMALL BOX WITH FLAP LID

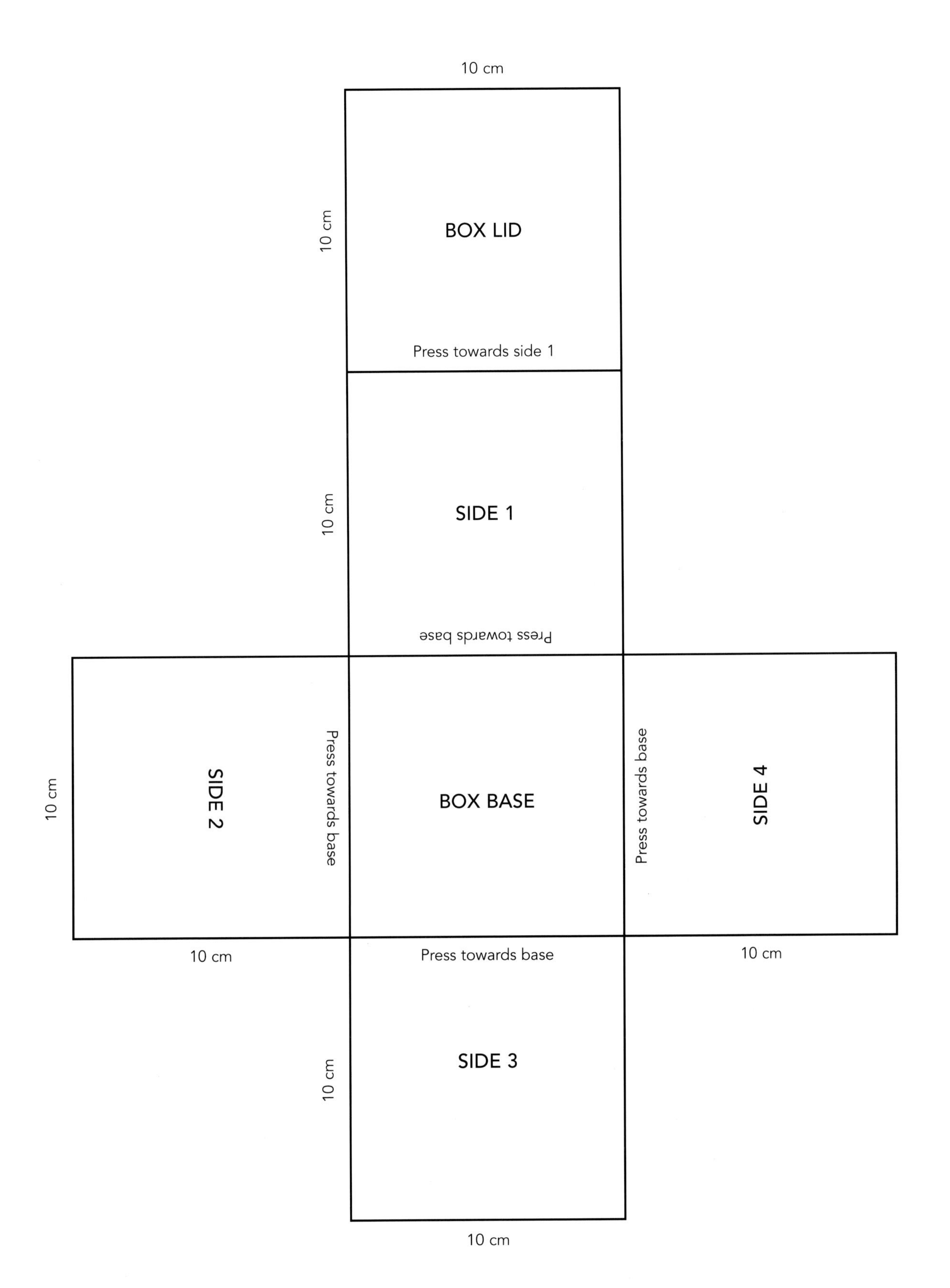

enlarge pattern by 200%

- Embellish with machine stitching (see 'Suggested Stitches for Mark Making' on page 48).

2. If you wish to embellish the lid you should do that now. Trying to stitch after you have sewn up the sides can be a bit tricky, although not impossible! You will find as you sew the silk 'paper' that it is not as flexible as fabric.
3. If you use a label on your work, stitch this on now, either on the inside or underside of the base, or inside the lid.
4. Should you find, at this stage, that the box needs to be more rigid, you can add some more Acrylic Gloss.
   - Lay the flat box on a thick pad of newspapers and brush on more adhesive over the box and over the embellishment on both sides.
   - Leave it to dry for six to eight hours or overnight. Using a hairdryer will leave the 'paper' quite stiff, and will cut down on the drying time.
5. Once dry, stitch up the four sides. This will be more difficult than sewing fabric but take it slowly and you will be delighted with the results. Push long pins through the two sides to be stitched. This is enough to enable the sides to be held together for stitching.
6. Start from the top of the box and stitch slowly down to the base, joining the four sides but leaving the lid free.
7. Embellish the lid with a tassel, a water-soluble motif or some machine made cords that have been twisted with wire and stitched on by hand.
8. When you have finished stitching, return the machine to general sewing mode.

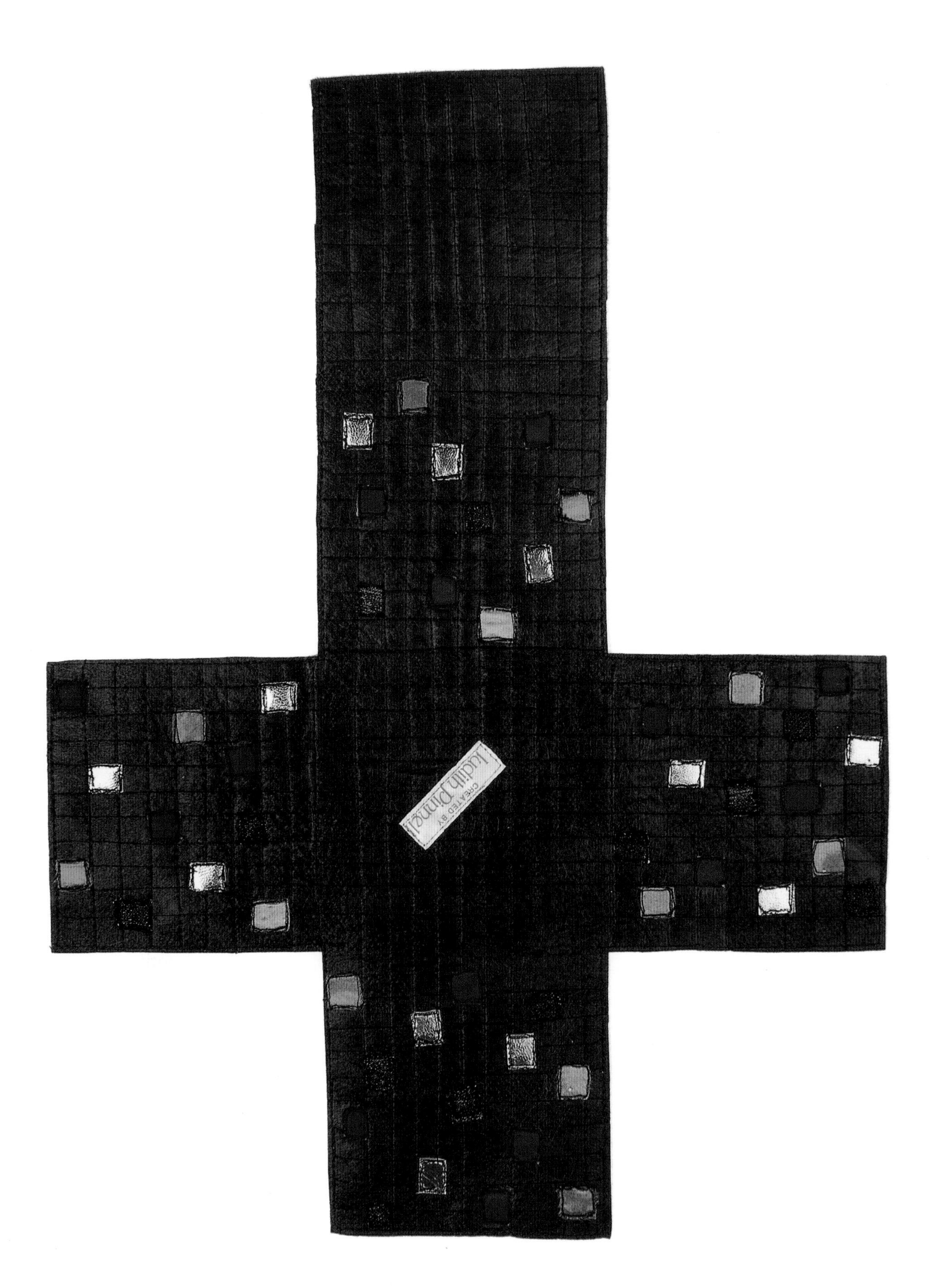
CREATED BY
Judith Pinnell

Theatre Purse

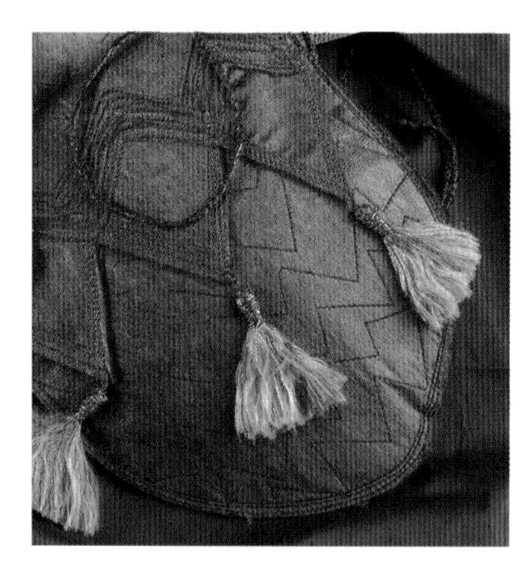

OPPOSITE & ABOVE: A selection of beaded and stitched Theatre Purses. Hand dyed tassels and beads are used to embellish some of the designs

This basic pattern can be varied to suit many shapes. You can add extra interest to your purse by attaching a tassel to either side of the top or bottom.

Materials

- A sheet of silk 'paper' at least 20″ x 28″ (50 cm x 70 cm) made with Textile Medium. Three layers work best for this projects.
- The 'paper' should be pressed before you begin to work with it.
- Thin Vilene or heavy paper to cut the pattern
- Your choice of machine embroidery threads (plain or metallic)
- Machine needles, size 10–12 (70 or 80)
- Sewing machine, open embroidery foot or pressure foot
- Long, sharp pins
- Sharp paper cutting scissors
- Embroidery scissors with sharp points
- Lining, silk or satin 16″ x 16″ (40 cm x 40 cm) (optional)
- Trimming: ornamental braids, ribbon, silk fabric
- For the shoulder cord: textured wool (not too thick), very thin ribbon—rayon or silk, cottons similar to DMC, 'glitz' threads like Twilley's Goldfinger in colours to tone or contrast with the 'paper' (you will use 4 or 5 lengths 42½″ or 108 cm long.)

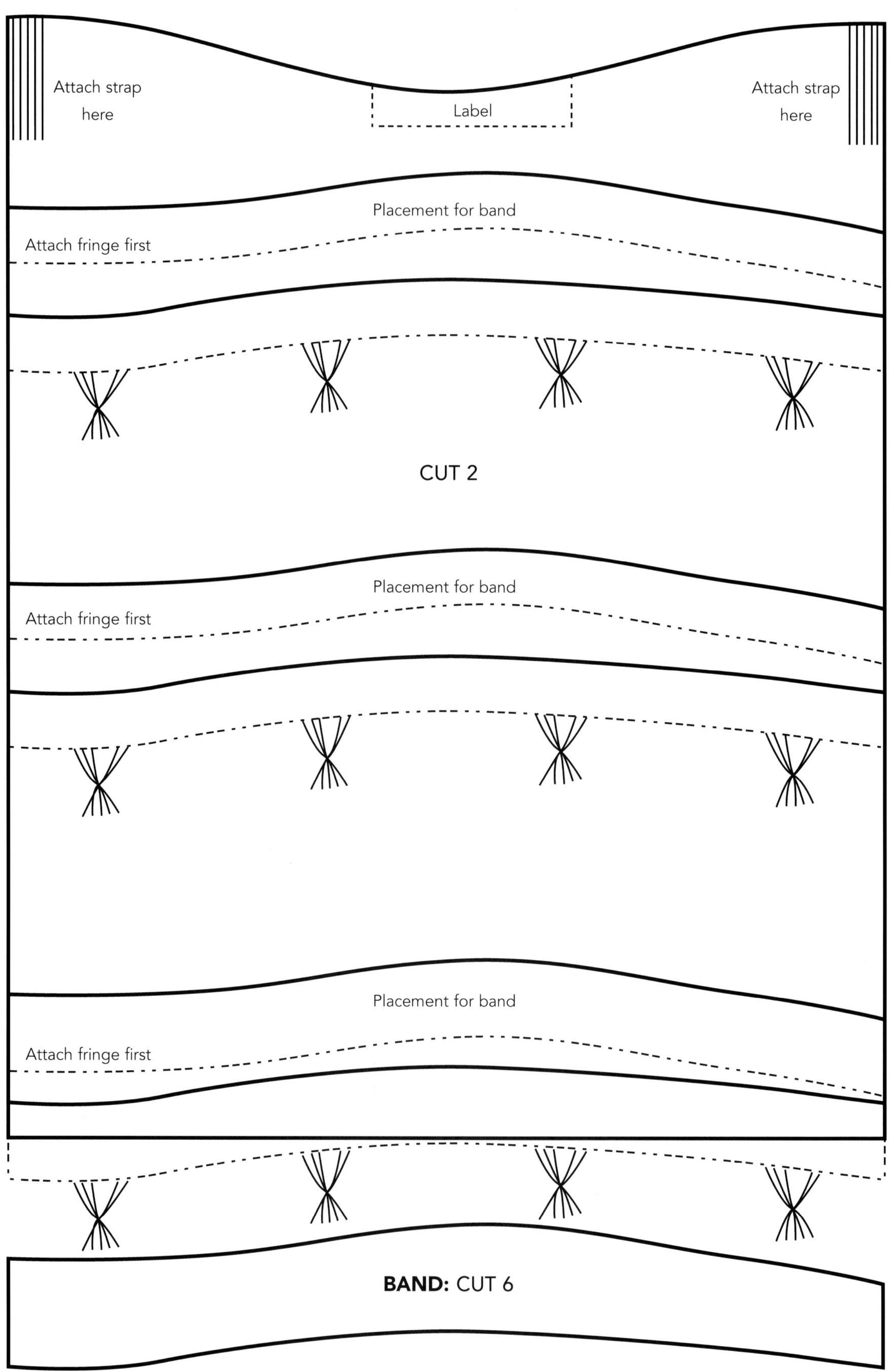

enlarge pattern by 111%

Method

1. Using the pattern as a guide cut out a pattern in Vilene or heavy paper.
2. Using sharp scissors cut one front, one back and six bands.
3. Use a new needle in the machine 10–12 (size 70 or 80 but no larger). Sew with an open embroidery foot if you have one, otherwise use the presser foot.
4. Thread the machine with machine embroidery thread on the top and in the bobbin. Slightly loosen the top tension to prevent the thread from breaking. Lengthen the stitch a little. Test the stitch length on a scrap of silk 'paper' before commencing to sew.
5. Stitch close to the outer edge on both sections of the purse and bands, to stabilise the edges of the silk 'paper'.

Theatre purse in construction shows placement for neck cord, label, and braid trim

Completed Theatre purse

6 You can either follow the surface decorations shown on the sample or embellish the purse with stitching. I have sewn a shape that follows the line of the top of the purse and stitched a furnishing braid underneath the applied shape.
7 Only the top of the shape and the braid have been sewn down leaving the lower edges free. See placement lines for shape and braid on pattern.
8 The surface decoration can be on both front and back, or on one side only.

The shoulder cord

1. Select four or five lengths of cord, ribbon or thread. Cut these into lengths about 43" (108 cm) long. The thickness of the cords/ribbons/threads will determine how many lengths you need, but the finished shoulder cord should not look too heavy. Once the lengths have been stitched together they are very strong.
2. Lay the threads close together, blending the colours and textures.
3. Set the sewing machine to running stitch (no. 3 on the Bernina).
4. Use machine embroidery thread, metallic or plain (a combination of metallic on top and plain in the bobbin can be effective).
5. The stitch width will automatically be at the widest when using the running stitch. Make the stitch length a little longer so that the stitching does not cover too much of the cords/ribbons/threads. You will need to test the stitch before starting to sew.
6. Pull out about 6" (15 cm) of machine threads.
7. Place the cords/ribbons threads together beneath the machine foot holding them taut. Sew along the cords/ribbons/threads, pulling the stitched end (at the back of the machine) gently away from you and at the same time steadying the unstitched cords at the front. You can sew them flat or gently twist as you sew.
8. When you have sewn the desired length of the cord, cut the machine threads off.
9. The running stitch will secure the threads but, if you wish to be sure they are secure, you can sew a couple of reverse stitches. Cut off excess cords/ribbons/threads. This makes a very firm shoulder cord.
10. Return the machine to straight stitch.

Sewing in your label

If you wish to sew in a label, do this now. Sew it to the centre of the inside of the purse or just inside the top edge of any lining you use as indicated on the pattern.

Attaching the shoulder cord

Stitch the shoulder cord approximately 1″ (2.5 cm) down on the inside of the back as shown on the pattern. Sew very close to the edge, stitching up and down three or four times using a straight stitch to secure the cord. Ensure that the cords do not protrude over the edge of the purse. Trim away any excess threads inside the purse.

Front to back

Pin the front to the back. Stitch sides together using machine embroidery thread, sewing two or three times all around for added strength. The seams will be on the outside of the purse, making them an integral part of the design.

Lining

Should you wish to line the purse, cut out a front and back remembering to allow at least ⅝″ (1.5 cm) all around for seams. Do not make the lining too tight for the purse—allow a little slack. Make up the lining, turning in the top edge by machine. Hand stitch the lining to the inside top edge of the purse. If you are using raw silk, it is a good idea to sew French seams to prevent any fraying of the silk fabric.

Contributing artists

Kristen Dibbs

Sydney, New South Wales

Necklace

18″ x 13½″ (45 cm x 34 cm)

Silk 'paper', decorated with machine embroidery and hand beading.

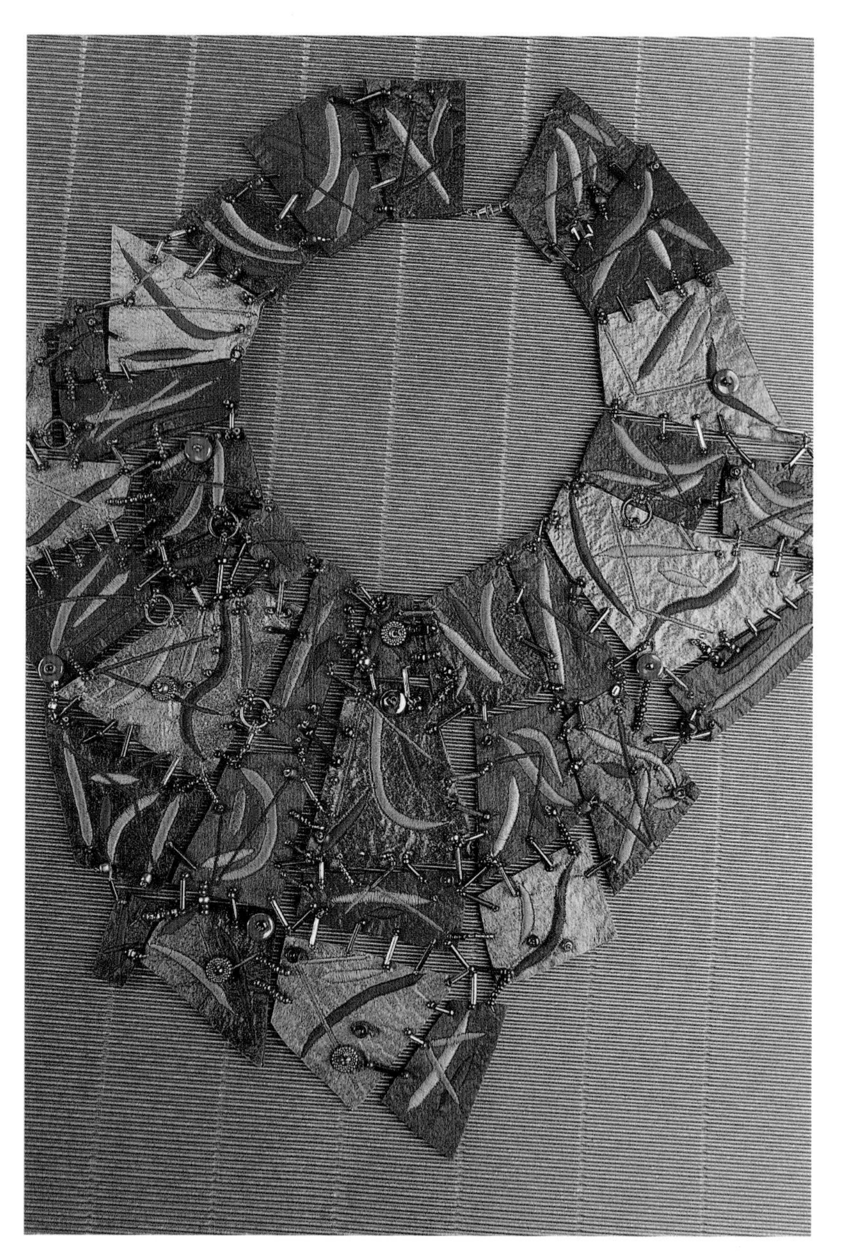

Other techniques used by the artist include: all forms of machine embroidery, combined with fabric manipulation; embroidery on soluble fabrics; and hand beading. These techniques are used to create artworks, garments, jewellery and accessories.

Lois Ives

Perth, Western Australia

Orange Potpourri Sachet

7½" x 6¾" (19 cm x 17 cm)

Silk 'paper', decorated with machine-made lace flowers, beads and Japanese braiding (kumihimo).

Lois makes accessories of silk 'paper', silk/felt and felt. Her favourite methods of decorating these accessories are needle-lace, beads, hand and machine embroidery. She also makes her own machine-made laces and braids. Besides sewing, kumihimo is her other big love. Currently she is experimenting with combining braid, needle-lace and beads into necklaces and bracelets.

Celia Player

Sydney, New South Wales

Untitled

25½" x 10½" (64 cm x 26 cm)

Freehand machine embroidery, hand painted fabrics and silk 'paper'

Other techniques used by the artist include: drawing; painting; mixed media techniques including collage, paper and fabric; hand stitching; and freehand machine embroidery

Thyra Robertson

Perth, Western Australia

Fragment

22" x 27.5" (55 cm x 69 cm)

Hand embroidery on a silk 'paper' background. Silk 'paper' has proved to be ideal for handwork. The silk 'paper' is good tempered enough to be used 'in the hand' without the use of an embroidery frame. Techniques used include: goldwork, chain and herringbone stitch, french knots, variations on couching and some ribbons. These have all been embellished with sequins and many kinds of beads.

In the past Thyra has enjoyed many of the traditional and non-traditional hand embroidery techniques. Today she likes to experiment, by combining all of the above techniques and using a variety of backgrounds, which she feels contribute to the successful interpretation of a design. She finds great pleasure in the slow but steady progress of hand embroidery.

Dale Rollerson

Perth, Western Australia

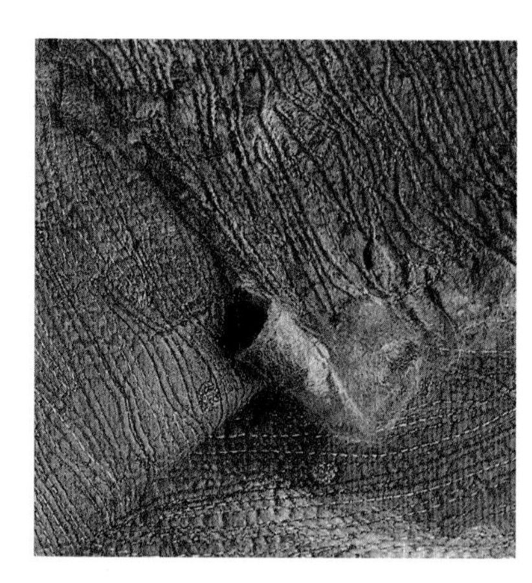

Stitch Magic

Straight stitch and twin needling on silk 'paper'

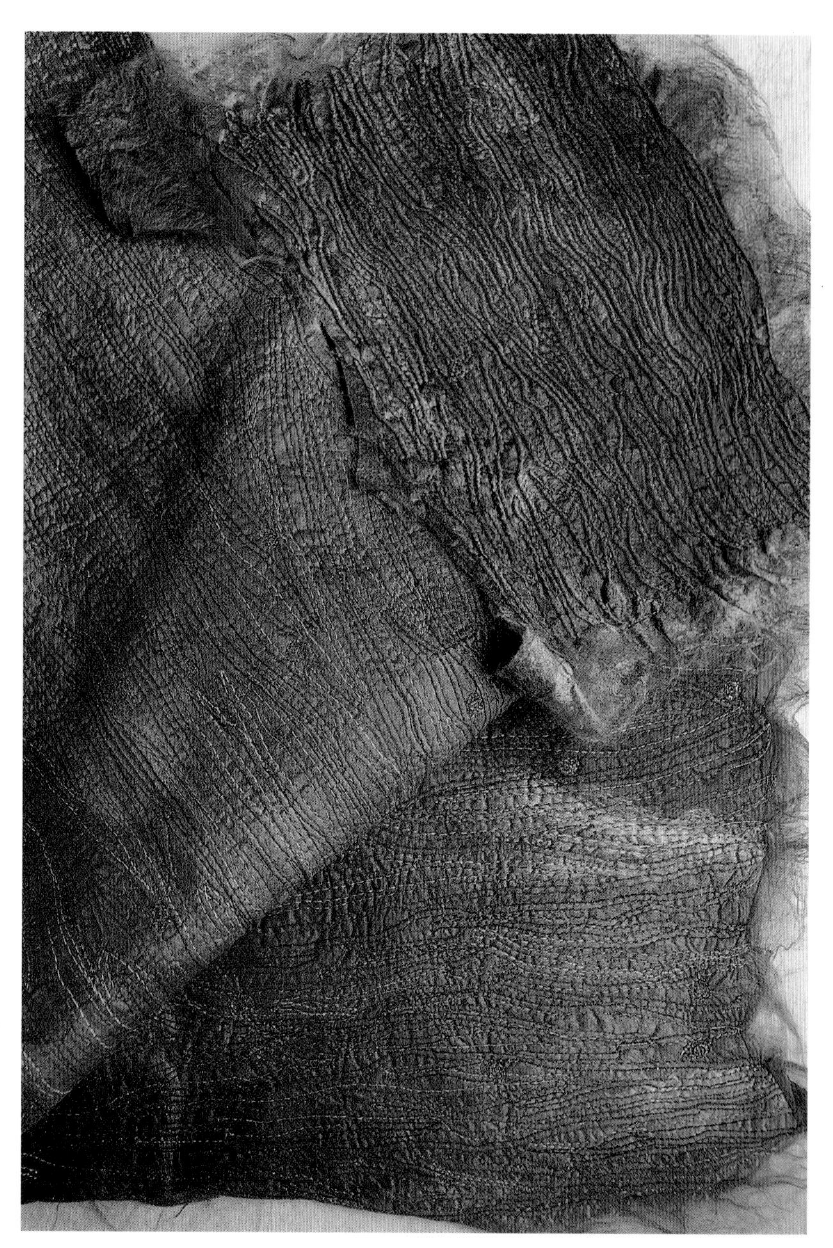

Dale is particularly interested in experimentation and exploring mixed media activities to incorporate with machine embroidery. She likes to play with colour and texture, and makes extensive use of working with soluble fabrics.

Karen Selk

Victoria, BC Canada

Magical Mobile

Three layers of silk fibre embellished with beadwork and a variety of stitches in hand and machine embroidery.

Karen Selk designs and weaves elegant silk clothing, and makes fused silk felt for wearable accessories and home decoration. She shares her approach through lectures and workshops.

Karen is co-owner of Treenway Silks where she designs yarns and accesses new products with Asian suppliers. She travels extensively through Asia researching the history, culture and heritage of silk traditions. She leads tours introducing others to the experiences of Asia. Karen also publishes her experiences in magazines.

Glossary

baking paper
Paper used for non-stick baking. This offers excellent visibility when tracing designs and is very strong.

batt/bat
A layer or layers of silk or wool fibres.

batting
Cotton, wool or polyester fibre used to interline fabrics for warmth and also to assist in texturing the surface when stitching is used.

couching
Threads, cords and wools that are too thick to be threaded through the machine needle are applied to the background material by means of a finer thread. The stitching thread can tone or contrast with the cord being couched. A long zigzag or serpentine stitch works well, or a straight stitch can be used if the couched cord is wide enough to straight stitch over.

cutting mat
The type with a self-sealable surface used in quilting. Use a very sharp craft knife to cut continuous lines on the silk 'paper'.

darning foot
This foot has a spring mechanism, which moves up and down with the needle, making it possible to stitch freely in any direction. There is also an open darning foot, which has a cut out section in the front that gives good visibility when sewing.

drying frame
The frame used to dry the wet silk. A constructed frame similar to that used for screen-printing is used to dry big pieces of silk 'paper'. When making small pieces, a cake cooling rack is suitable.

free machine embroidery
By using the darning foot or no foot at all and dropping the feed teeth or not as you wish, you have complete control over the direction and size of the stitch. When free machining, conventional fabrics need to be worked in a machine embroidery frame, but the beauty of silk 'paper' is that it can be worked without a frame.

medium
The solution used to bond the raw silk fibres together.

open embroidery foot
This foot is similar to the presser foot but has a wide opening at the front that makes it easier to view the stitching. I use it with most of my sewing.

'paper'
refers to silk 'paper'.

substrate
The base fabric, an under layer.

tops
A thick rope-like mass of parallel fibres in either wool or silk.

trace and stitch
A method used to apply a design to a background. Trace the design on to transparent paper, tack the paper to the background fabric and machine or hand stitch around the design. Carefully tear away the paper. Stubborn pieces can be removed with tweezers.

Velcro
The trade name for a two-component fastening. One strip has fine plastic 'teeth'—the other strip has a 'furry' surface that enables the 'teeth' to adhere to it. This can be purchased in various widths and colours from sewing centres.

Vliesofix
The trade name for paper-backed, double-sided, fusible webbing.

Suppliers

Nancy Ballesteros Trading as
'Treetops colour Harmonies'
6 Benwee Road
Floreat 6014
Western Australia
Tel: (08) 9387 3007
Fax: (08) 9387 1747
email: treetops@perth.dialix.oz.au
www.treetopscolours.com.au
Supplier of dyed silk tops and Acrylic Gloss Medium/Varnish and Textile Medium

Treenway Silks
725 Caledonia Avenue
Victoria, B.C. V8T 1E4
Canada
Toll Free 1-883-383-SILK
Tel: (250) 383 1661
email: treenway@coastnet.com
Supplier of dyed silk tops

Sue Hiley Silks
Sue Hiley Harris
The Mill, Tregoyd Mill
Three Cocks, Brecon
Powys, LD3 OSW
United Kingdom
Tel/Fax: 01497 847421
email: suesilk@btinternet.com
Supplier of dyed silk tops

Martien Van Zuilen
28 Seaview Street
Beaconsfield WA 6162
Australia
Tel: (08) 9335 5696
Supplier of dyed silk tops

Chroma Distributors

Suppliers of Textile Medium and Acrylic Gloss Medium

Chroma Australia Pty Ltd
17 Mundowi Road
Mt Kuring-gai NSW 2080
Australia

Tomas Seth & Co Ltd
Tomas Seth Business Park
Argent Road, Queenborough
Sheppey, Kent ME11 5JP
United Kingdom

Chroma Inc.
205 Bucky Drive
Lititz, PA 17543
USA